LEARN
PYTHON
FAST

This Book Includes:

Python Programming

and Machine Learning

The Complete Starter Guide for Total Beginners +
Practical Exercises

Computer Programming Academy

Table of Contents

Introduction to Python Programming: Week 1

Python Programming: An hands-on introduction to computer programming and algorithms, a project-based guide with practical exercises

The following chapters will discuss various fundamental concepts of the Python programming language. There are 7 chapters in this book, crafted specifically to help you master basic and advanced python programming concepts required to develop web based programs and applications in just a week.

The first chapter of this book starts with an introduction to computer programming and some of the most widely used programming languages. You will also learn the fundamental elements of computer programming language such as basic operators, functions, decision making, among others. The importance of mathematical concepts such as algebra and statistics in computer programming has also been explained. Chapter 2 will provide a detailed overview of Python and its historical development. Step by step instructions to install Python on your operating systems have also been included. The concept of Python comments, variables and data types that serve as a prerequisite to the learning of Python programming have been explained in detail.

Chapter 3 is a detailed overview of the basic concepts of Python programming focusing on various programming elements such as Booleans, Tuples, Sets, Dictionaries and much more. The nuances of how to write efficient and effective Python codes have been explained in detail along with plenty of examples and sample exercises to help you solidify your understanding of these concepts. Chapter 4 pertains to the advance Python programming concepts that are relatively more complicated and require a solid understanding of the basic concepts. You will learn how to use OOPS concepts, different loops and conditional statements to generate sophisticated commands. This chapter also includes plenty of examples and sample exercises so you can verify what you have learned. Like most programming languages, Python boasts a number of built-in functions to make your life easier while coding a software program. Chapter 5 contains a list of all such built-in functions, methods and keywords that can be used to easily develop and run advance codes. Chapter 6 will provide a detailed overview of Django which is web framework that is popularly used in the development of web based programs and applications. You will learn how to install Django on your computer and follow the step by step coding instructions to develop your own web based program and notes taking application.

The final chapter, "Python Applications", will provide details on how Python programming is being used in the development and testing of software programs, machine learning algorithms and Artificial Intelligence technologies to solve real world problems. These cutting edge technologies have resulted in tools and programs that are being utilized across the industrial spectrum to solve real world problems and become more futuristic. This chapter also includes various Python programming tips and tricks that will help you take your coding skills to the next level.

2

Day 1: Computer Programming 101

Humans have evolved their medium of communication over centuries, resulting in a wide variety of languages spoken across the world. However, all manmade languages have a shared set of features that are remarkably standard across the board. Every language has a script containing different parts of a structured sentence such as nouns, verbs, adjectives, and other elements.

This is where we can draw a bridge to the computer programming languages, which are also composed of a variety of fundamental elements. We will look at each of these elements in detail later in this chapter. However, computer languages allow humans to interact with and guide the computing machines to perform desired operations. It allows the development and implementation of advance computing technologies. These programming languages also allow computers to interact with one another.

Here is a quick overview of some of the most popular computer programming languages.

C

C Language can be defined as a structure-oriented (functions are stored as a self-contained unit), medium level programming language widely utilized in the development of "low-level" applications (pertaining to hardware components of the computer). In 1972, Bell Laboratories developed the C language for implementation in the UNIX system. A number of sophisticated and advanced programming languages such as Java, JavaScript, C++, C# and Perl are derived from the "grandmother" C language. Until the introduction of Java, the C language was the most dominant high-level language of the industry. Some of the only operating systems like IBM System/370 were also developed using the C language.

The C language is rated low on the scale of learning difficulty primarily owing to the limited number of keywords,32, that need to be trained on, and thus, it often serves as a foundational language for coding beginners. It is often used for the development of software applications that require integration to an operating system like UNIX, Linux and Windows. Some of the most popular C language based applications are: Word processors, OS development, database systems, network drivers and interpreters, compilers and assemblers, spreadsheets and graphics packages. Facebook's TAO systems are developed using the C language.

C++

Developed in 1983 as an extension of the C language, C++ can be defined as an object oriented (grouping of function and the associated dataset into an object), "medium level" (interacting with the programming layer of the computer) programming language that can be used for the development of general purpose software. It allows coding in similar syntax as the C language making C++ a perfect example of a "hybrid language". The C++ language with a robust standard library and (STL) quick processing and compilation mechanism, is used to develop various application suites such as "Microsoft Office", graphics editing tools, video editors, gaming packages and even entire Operating Systems. The "BlackBerry" operating system and the latest Microsoft Office suite are developed entirely on the C++ language.

The C++ language is widely perceived as the enhanced version of the C language with object oriented up to approach that can be used to generate efficient and lean code. It also provides a high level of abstraction to allow improved management of large development projects. The C++ language tends to be the first programming language taught at college level. Some of the major companies and organizations using C++ are Amazon, Google, Adobe software, Mozilla, Winamp, and Lockheed Martin. The C++ language is specifically used in the development of Embedded Firmware, Client Server Applications, Drivers, and system programs.

C#

In 2000, Microsoft released C# (pronounced as C-sharp) as part of its .Net framework, which was developed using other languages like C, C++, and Java as a foundational basis. In 2003, C# became an ISO certified multi-paradigm programming language with powerful features including high functionality, object oriented, imperativeness, declarative attributes and component orientation. Developers use C# a lot to write codes for the XML web services applications as well as Applications connected with Microsoft .Net for the Windows Operating System. The C# language is the go to programming language for Microsoft applications and the language of choice for the Windows Presentation Foundation (WPF). With the introduction of .Net Standard and .Net Core, the .Net ecosystem evolved into cross-platform frameworks and standards, capable of running on Windows, Linux and Mac. The C# language is ideal for beginners and has similar capabilities as Java. It is a high level programming language with high similarity to the English language reading, making it easy to learn and use. It is still not as high level and easy to learn for beginners as Python. Game development is another population application for the C# language, said to be the language of choice to develop and enhance games on the "Unity Game Engine". Developers can write android and iOS applications in C# using Microsoft Xamarin framework.

Java

Java, now owned by Oracle, was introduced in 1991 by Sun Microsystems as a high-level, memory managed language called "Oak" to add capabilities to the C++ language. It is the leading development language and framework with features like general-purpose, object-oriented making it ideal for web based application development. Java runs on the principle of WORA (Write Once Run Anywhere) and has cross-platform capability, making it ideal for developing mobile and gaming applications at the enterprise level.

The Java Server Pages (JSP) is used to develop web based applications. Java allows applications to be accessed through a browser and easily downloadable. The Java byte code is compiled from the Java language and runs on the Java Virtual Machine (JVM). These JVMs are available for a majority of operating systems like Windows and Mac. Some programs that are developed using Java are Eclipse, Lotus Notes, Minecraft, Adobe Creative Suite and open office. Google's Android operating system and app development are primarily driven by Java. It is a robust and interpreted language with

6

high application portability, extensive network library and automatic memory management.

JavaScript

Due to a similarity in the name, people often assume that there is an underlying connection to Java, but it's far from the truth. JavaScript was developed in 1995 by the company Netscape and called "LiveScript". JavaScript processes commands on the computer instead of a server and runs inside a client browser. It is primarily used in web development to make webpages more dynamic and manipulate various elements such as: creating a calendar functionality, printing time and date, adding webpage scrolling abilities and other features that cannot be developed using plain HTML.

Web server called NodeJS runs entirely on JavaScript on the server-side. JavaScript is frequently used by front-end web developers and game developers in a variety of domains such as marketing, information technology, engineering, healthcare and finance. A British agency called Cyber-Duck was developed with JavaScript and uses public APIs to access data concerning crime and enable authorities to review and safeguard local areas. Pete Smart and Robert Hawkes created "Tweetmap", that serves as a depiction of the world map in proportion to the number of "tweets" generated by each country. The fundamental features of JavaScript are considered relatively easy to understand and master. A comprehensive JavaScript library called "JQuery" containing multiple frameworks is widely used by the developers as reference.

Python

Python first introduced in 1989 and is touted as extremely user-friendly and easy to learn programming language for amateurs and entry level coders. It is considered perfect for people who have newly taken up interest in programming or coding and need to understand the fundamentals of programming. This emanates from the fact that Python reads almost like English language. Therefore, it requires less time to understand how the language works and focus can be directed in learning the basics of programming.

Here are some of the fundamental elements of computer programming language:

- **Data Type** – This concept is applicable to every programming language ever designed. The data type is simply a representation of the type of data that needs to be processed by the computer. Some of the most common data types are string, numeric, alphanumeric, decimals, among others. Each programming language has its own definition of the data types and keywords used to write the code. For example, the keyword "char" is used to define string data type in C and Java.

- **Variable** – Data values can be stored on a computer by specifying desired label or name to select computer memory locations. These labels are referred to as variables. For instance, you can store values like "Christmas is on" and "12/25" using variables like "A" and "B" and then subsequently execute scientific program to retrieve desired output. Every programming language will have unique keywords and syntax to create and use required variables.

- **Keywords** – Each programming language has a basic syntax with certain words reserved to indicate specific meaning and cannot be used to create variable names. For example, C programming language used words like "int" and "float" to indicate data types; therefore, you will not be able to create variables named "int" or "float".

- **Basic Operators** – Programming language operators refer to symbols that inform the program compiler to perform the indicated mathematical, logical or relational operation and produce desired output. For example, the arithmetic operator "+" in C programming language will execute the addition command on indicated values. Similarly, relational operator ">" will allow you to compare data values and generate true or false result.

- **Decision Making** – This element pertains to selection of one of the provided options on the basis of the provided conditions. For instance, if a remark needs to be printed, the programming code needs to include one or more required conditional statements that will be processed through the workflow of the program. "If" and "If else" conditional statements are some of the decision making statements used in C and Python.

- **Functions** – A set of reusable and organized code that can be utilized to execute a related action is called as function. They offer enhanced modularity for the app and more reusability of the code. For instance, built in functions like "main ()" or "printf ()" can be written and used in C programming language. Different languages refer to functions using different terminologies like subroutine, method, or procedure.

- **File I/O** – Data values can be stored in various formats such as images, plain texts, rich media, and more using computer files. You can organize these files into distinct directories. In short, files hold data and directories hold files. For instance , the extension ".c" will be added to the end of C programming files and extension ".java" to all Java files. The input files can be created in text editing tools like MS Word or Notepad and output files allows reading of the data from the file. The output files are used to show the results on the screen by executing the input to the program from the command prompt.

Importance of Mathematics in Computer Programming

The discipline of mathematics is extremely important to learn and understand the fundamental concepts of computer programming. Various concepts of "Discrete Mathematics", such as probability, algebra, set theory, logic notation, among others, are intricate parts of computer programming. Algebra is frequently used in programming languages. For example, "Boolean Algebra" can be utilized in logical operations and "Relational Algebra" can be utilized

10

in databases. Another example is used of "Number Theory" in the development of cryptocurrency.

Computer science algorithms, including machine learning algorithms, consist of a set of instructions required in the implementation of an application or program. A basic algorithm is as simple as a mathematics statement written using logical operator "+" (5+7 = 12) to code for the addition of data values. The whole concept of data analysis and problem solving is dependent on the mathematical equations that are analyzed to understand the crux of an error. By addressing those issues directly using the mathematics of the program, hard fixes can be easily made to the application.

Statistics is also widely used in data mining and compression, as well as speech recognition and image analysis software. The field of Artificial Intelligence and Machine Learning share a lot of core concepts from the field of statistics. "Statistical learning" is a descriptive statistics-based learning framework that can be categorized as supervised or unsupervised. "Supervised statistical learning" includes constructing a statistical model to predict or estimate output based on single or multiple inputs, on the other hand, "unsupervised statistical learning" involves inputs but no supervisory output, but helps in learning data relationships and structure. One way of understanding statistical learning is to identify the connection between the "predictor" (autonomous variables, attributes) and the "response" (autonomous variable), in order to produce a specific model which is capable of predicting the "response variable (Y)" on the basis of "predictor factors (X)".

"X = f(X) + ε where X = (X1,X2, . . .,Xp)", where "f" is an *"unknown function"* & "ε" is *"random error (reducible & irreducible)"*.

If there are a number of inputs "X" easily accessible, but the output "B" production is unknown, "f" is often treated as a black box, provided that it generates accurate predictions for "Y". This is called "prediction". There are circumstances in which we need to understand how "Y" is influenced as "X" changes. We want to estimate "f" in this scenario, but our objective is not simply to generate predictions for "Y". In this situation, we want to establish and better understand the connection between "Y" and "X". Now "f" is not regarded as a black box since we have to understand the underlying process of the system. This is called "inference". In everyday life, various issues can be categorized into the setting of "predictions", the setting of "inferences", or a "hybrid" of the two.

The "parametric technique" can be defined as an evaluation of "f" by calculating the set parameters (finite summary of the data) while establishing an assumption about the functional form of "f". The mathematical equation of this technique is *"f(X) = β0 + β1X1 + β2X2 + . . . + βpXp"*. The "parametric models" tend to have a finite number of parameters which is independent of the size of the data set. This is also known as "model-based learning". For example, "k-Gaussian models" are driven by parametric techniques.

On the other hand, the "non-parametric technique" generates an estimation of "f" on the basis of its closeness to the data points, without making any assumptions on the functional form of "f". The "non-parametric models" tend to have a varying number of parameters, which grows proportionally with the size of the data set. This is also known as "memory-based learning". For example, "kernel density models" are driven by a non-parametric technique.

Day 2: Introduction to Python

Python is a high-level programming language, commonly used for general purposes. It was originally developed by Guido van Rossum at the "Center Wiskunde & Informatica (CWI), Netherlands", in the 1980s and introduced by the "Python Software Foundation" in 1991. It was designed primarily to emphasize the readability of programming code, and its syntax enables programmers to convey ideas using fewer lines of code. Python programming language increases the speed of operation while allowing for higher efficiency in creating system integrations. Developers are using Python for "web development (server-side), software development, mathematics, system scripting".

With the introduction of various enhancements such as "list comprehension" and a "garbage collection system", which can collect reference cycles, the Python 2.0 was launched in the last quarter of 2000. Subsequently, in 2008, Python 3.0 was released as a major version upgrade with backward compatibility allowing for the Python 2.0 code to be executed on Python 3.0 without requiring any modifications. Python is supported by a community of programmers that continually develop and maintain the "CPython", which is an open-source reference implementation. The "Python Software Foundation" is a not for profit organization that is responsible for managing and directing resources for developing Python programming as well as "CPython".

Here are some of the key features of Python that render it as the language of choice for coding beginners as well as advanced software programmers alike:

1. **Readability**: Python reads a lot like the English language, which contributes to its ease of readability.

2. **Learnability**: Python is a high level programming language and considered easy to learn due to the ability to code using English language like expressions, which implies it is simple to comprehend and thereby learn the language.

3. **Operating Systems**: Python is easily accessible and can be operated across different Operating systems, including Linux, Unix, Mac, Windows among others. This renders Python as a versatile and cross-platform language.

4. **Open Source**: Python is "open source", which means that the developer community can seamlessly make updates to the code, which are always available to anyone using Python for their software programming needs.

5. **Standardized Data Libraries**: Python features a big standard data library with a variety of useful codes and functionalities that can be used when writing Python code for data analysis and development of machine learning models. (Details on machine learning libraries will be provided later in this chapter)

6. **Free**: Considering the wide applicability and usage of Python, it is hard to believe that it continues to be freely available for easy download and use. This implies that anyone looking to learn or use Python can simply download and use it for their applications completely free of charge. Python is indeed a perfect example of a "FLOSS (Free/Libre Open

Source Software)", which means one could "freely distribute copies of this software, read its source code and modify it".

7. **Supports managing of exceptions**: An "exception" can be defined as "an event that can occur during program exception and can disrupt the normal flow of program". Python is capable of supporting handling of these "exceptions", implying that you could write fewer error-prone codes and test your code with a variety of cases, which could potentially lead to an "exception" in the future.

8. **Advanced Features**: Python can also support "generators and list comprehensions". **Storage governance**: Python is also able to support "automatic memory management", which implies that the storage memory will be cleared and made available automatically. You are not required to clear and free up the system memory.

Installation Instructions for Python

You can follow the step by step instructions to download and install Python on a variety of operating systems. Simply jump to the section for the operating system you are working on. The latest version of Python released in the middle of the 2019 is Python 3.8.0. Make sure you are downloading and installing the most recent and stable version of Python and following the instructions below.

WINDOWS

1. From the official Python website, click on the "Downloads" icon and select Windows.

2. Click on the "Download Python 3.8.0" button to view all the downloadable files.

3.   You will be taken to a different screen where you can select the Python version you would like to download. In this book, we will be using the Python 3 version under "Stable Releases". So scroll down the page and click on the "Download Windows x86-64 executable installer" link, as shown in the picture below.

- Python 3.8.0 - Oct. 14, 2019

  Note that Python 3.8.0 *cannot* be used on Windows XP or earlier.

  - Download Windows help file
  - Download Windows x86-64 embeddable zip file
  - Download Windows x86-64 executable installer
  - Download Windows x86-64 web-based installer
  - Download Windows x86 embeddable zip file
  - Download Windows x86 executable installer
  - Download Windows x86 web-based installer

4.   A pop-up window titled "python-3.8.0-amd64.exe" will be displayed.

5.   Click on the "Save File" button to start downloading the file.

6.   Once the download has completed, double click the saved file icon, and a "Python 3.8.0 (64-bit) Setup" pop window will be displayed.

7.   Make sure that you select the "Install Launcher for all users (recommended)" and the "Add Python 3.8 to PATH" checkboxes. Note – If you already have an older version of Python installed on your system, the "Upgrade Now" button

will appear instead of the "Install Now" button, and neither of the checkboxes will be displayed.

8. Click on the "Install Now" button and a "User Account Control" pop up window will be displayed.

9. A notification stating, "Do you want to allow this app to make change to your device" will be displayed, click on Yes.

10. A new pop up window titled "Python 3.8.0 (64-bit) Setup" will be displayed containing a setup progress bar.

11. Once the installation has been completed, a "Set was successful" message will be displayed. Click on the Close button, and you are all set.

12. To verify the installation, navigate to the directory where you installed Python and double click on the python.exe file.

MACINTOSH

1. From the official Python website, click on the "Downloads" icon and select Mac.

2. Click on the "Download Python 3.8.0" button to view all the downloadable files.

3. You will be taken to a different screen where you can select the Python version you would like to download. In this book, we will be using the Python 3 version under "Stable Releases". So scroll down the page and click on the "Download macOS 64-bit installer" link under Python 3.8.0, as shown in the picture below.

- Python 3.7.5 - Oct. 15, 2019
  - Download macOS 64-bit/32-bit installer
  - Download macOS 64-bit installer
- Python 3.8.0 - Oct. 14, 2019
  - Download macOS 64-bit installer
- Python 3.7.4 - July 8, 2019
  - Download macOS 64-bit/32-bit installer
  - Download macOS 64-bit installer
- Python 3.6.9 - July 2, 2019

4. A pop-up window titled "python-3.8.0-macosx10.9.pkg" will be displayed.

5. Click on the "Save File" button to start downloading the file.

6. Once the download has completed, double click the saved file icon, and an "Install Python" pop window will be displayed.

7. Click on the "Continue" button to proceed, and a terms and conditions pop up window will be displayed.

8. Click Agree and then click on the "Install" button.

9. A notification requesting administrator permission and password will be displayed. Simply enter your system password to begin installation.

10. Once the installation has been completed, an "Installation was successful" message will be displayed. Click on the Close button, and you are all set.

11. To verify the installation, navigate to the directory where you installed Python and double click on the python launcher icon that will take you to the Python Terminal.

LINUX

- **For Red Hat, CentOS, or Fedora**, install the python3 and python3-devel packages.
- **For Debian or Ubuntu**, install the python3.x and python3.x-dev packages.
- **For Gentoo**, install the '=python-3.x*' ebuild (you may have to unmask it first).

1. From the official Python website, click on the "Downloads" icon and select Linux/UNIX.

2. Click on the "Download Python 3.8.0" button to view all the downloadable files.

3. You will be taken to a different screen where you can select the Python version you would like to download. In this book, we will be using the Python 3 version under "Stable Releases". So scroll down the page and click on the "Download Gzipped source tarball" link under Python 3.8.0, as shown in the picture below.

- Download Gzipped source tarball
- Download XZ compressed source tarball
- Python 3.8.0 - Oct. 14, 2019
  - Download Gzipped source tarball
  - Download XZ compressed source tarball
- Python 3.7.4 - July 8, 2019
  - Download Gzipped source tarball
  - Download XZ compressed source tarball

4.   A pop-up window titled "python-3.7.5.tgz" will be displayed.

5.   Click on the "Save File" button to start downloading the file.

6.   Once the download has completed, double click the saved file icon, and an "Install Python" pop window will be displayed.

7.   Follow the prompts on the screen to complete the installation process.

Getting Started

Now that you have the Python terminal installed on your computer, we will now see how you can start writing and executing the Python code. All Python codes are written in a text editor as (.py) files, which are then executed on the Python interpreter on the command line as shown in the code below, where "smallworld.py" is the name of the Python file:

"C: \Users\Your Name\python smallworld.py"

You can test a small code without writing the code in a file and simply executing it as a command-line itself by typing the code below on the Mac, Windows or Linux command line, as shown below:

"C: \Users\Your Name\python"

In case the above command doesn't work, you can use the code below instead

"C: \Users\Your Name\py"

21

Indentation – To understand the Python coding structure, you must first understand the significance of indentation or the number of spaces before you start typing the code. Unlike other coding languages where "indentation" is added to enhance the readability of the code, in Python, it is used to indicate a set of code. For example, look at the code below

If 7 > 4:

print ('Seven is greater than 4')

There is indentation prior to the second line of code with the print command. If you skip the indentation and write the code as below, you will receive an error:

If 7 > 4:

print ('Seven is greater than 4')

The number of spaces can be adjusted but must be at least single-spaced. For example, you can execute the code below with higher indentation, but for a specific set of code same number of spaces must be used, or you will receive an error.

If 7 > 4:

print ('Seven is greater than 4')

Adding Comments – In Python, you can add comments to the code by starting the code comment lines with a "#", as shown in the example below:

#Add any relevant comment here

print ('Planet Earth')

Comments are also used as a description of the code and not executed by the Python terminal. It is important to remember that if you put a comment at the end of code like the entire code line will be skipped by the Python terminal, as shown in the code below. Comments are extremely useful in case you need to stop the execution when you are testing the code.

print ('Planet Earth')   #Add comments here

You can also add multiple lines of comments by starting each code line with "#", as shown below:

#Add comment here
#Supplement the comment here
#Further add the comment here
print ('Planet Earth')

Python Variables

In Python, variables are used to store data values without executing a command for it. You can create a variable by simply assigning desired value to it, as shown in the example below:

A = 110
B = 'David'
print (A)
print (B)

A variable may be declared without a specific data type. The data type of a variable can also be modified after its initial declaration, as shown in the example below:

A = 110 # A has data type set as int

23

A = 'David' # A now has data type str

print (A)

There are certain rules applied to the Python variable names as follows:

    1.   Variable names can be short as single alphabets or more descriptive words like height, weight, etc

    2.   Variable names can only be started with an underscore character or a letter.

    3.   Variable names must not start with numbers.

    4.   Variable names may contain underscores or alphanumeric characters. No other special characters are allowed.

    5.   Variable names are case sensitive. For example, 'height,' 'Height' and 'HEIGHT' will be accounted as 3 separate variables.

Assigning Value to Variables

In Python, multiple variables can be assigned DISTINCT values in a single code line, as shown in the example below:

A, B, C = 'lilac,' 'red,' 'cyan'

print (A)

print (B)

print (C)

OR multiple variables can be assigned SAME value in a single code line, as shown in the example below:

A, B, C = 'lilac'

print (A)

print (B)

print (C)

Python Data Types

To further understand the concept of variables, let's first look at the Python data types. Python supports a variety of data types as listed below:

Category	Data Type	Example Syntax
Text	*"str"*	'Planet Earth' "Planet Earth" """Planet Earth"""
Boolean	*"bool"*	'True' 'False'
Mapping (mixed data types, associative array of key and value pairs)	*"dict"*	'{'key9' : 9.0, 6 : True}'
Sequence (may contain mixed data types)	*"list"*	'[9.0, 'character', True]'
	"tuple"	'[9.0, 'character,' True]'

25

	"range"	'range (10, 50)' 'range (100, 50, 10,-10,-50,-100)'
Binary	*"bytes"*	b 'byte sequence' b 'byte sequence' bytes ([120, 90, 75, 100])
	"bytearray"	bytearray (b 'byte sequence') bytearray (b 'byte sequence') bytearray ([120, 90, 75, 100])
	"memoryview"	
Set (unordered, no duplicates, mixed data types)	*"set"*	'[9.0, 'character,' True]'

	"frozenset"	'frozenset ([9.0, 'character', True])'
Numeric	*"int"*	'54'
	"float"	'18e9'
	"complex"	'18 + 3.1j'
Ellipsis (index in NumPy arrays)	*"ellipsis"*	'...' 'Ellipsis'

To view the data type of any object, you can use the *"type ()"* function as shown in the example below:

A = 'Lilac'

print (type (A))

Assigning the Data Type to Variables

As mentioned earlier, you can create a new variable by simply declaring a value for it. This set data value, in turn, assigns the data type to the variable. To assign a specific data type to a variable, the constructor functions listed below can be used:

Constructor Functions	Data Type
A = str ('Planet Earth)'	str
A = int (99)	Int (Must be a whole number, positive or negative with no decimals, no length restrictions)

A = float (15e6)	Float (Floating point number must be positive or negative with one or more decimals; maybe scientific number an 'e' to specify an exponential power of 10)
A = complex (99j)	Complex (Must be written with a 'j' as an imaginary character)
A = list (('cyan', 'red', 'olive'))	list
A = range (1, 100)	range
A = tuple (('cyan', 'red', 'olive'))	tuple
A = set (('cyan', 'red', 'olive'))	set
A = frozenset (('cyan', 'olive', 'red'))	frozenset
A = dict ('color' : 'red', 'year' : 1999)	dict
A = bool (False)	bool
A = bytes (54)	bytes
A = bytearray (8)	bytearray
A = memoryview (bytes (55))	memoryview

EXERCISE – To solidify your understanding of data types. Look at the first column of the table below and write the data type for that variable. Once you have all your answers, look at the second column, and verify your answers.

Variable	Data Type
A = 'Planet Earth'	str
A = 99	int
A = 29e2	float
A = 99j	complex
A = ['cyan', 'red,' 'olive']	list
A = range (1, 100)	range
A = ('cyan,' 'red,' 'olive')	tuple
A = {'cyan', 'red', 'olive'}	set
A = frozenset ({ 'cyan', 'olive', 'red'})	frozenset
A = ['color' : 'red', 'year' : 1999}	dict
A = False	bool
A = b 'Welcome'	bytes
A = bytearray (8)	bytearray
A = memoryview (bytes (55))	memoryview

Output Variables

In order to retrieve variables as output, the "print" statements are used in Python. You can use the "+" character to combine text with a variable for final output, as shown in the example below:

'A = 'red'

print ('Apples are' + A)'

OUTPUT – 'Apples are red'

A variable can also be combined with another variable using the "+" character, as shown in the example below:

'A = 'Apples are'

B = 'red'

AB = A + B

print (AB)'

OUTPUT – 'Apples are red'

However, when the "+" character is used with numeric values, it retains its function as a mathematical operator, as shown in the example below:

'A = 20

B = 30

print (A + B)'

OUTPUT = 50

You will not be able to combine a string of characters with numbers and will trigger an error instead, as shown in the example below:

A = 'red'

B = 30

print (A + B)

OUTPUT – N/A – ERROR

Day 3: Coding Basics

In the previous chapter, you learned the basics of Python syntax, the concept of Python Variables, and Comments that serve as a prerequisite to the learning of Python programming. In this chapter, we will be looking at the nuances of how to write efficient and effective Python codes, focusing on various programming elements such as Booleans, Tuples, Sets, Dictionaries and much more. So let's get started.

Python Numbers

In Python programming, you will be working with 3 different numeric data types, namely, "int", "float", and "complex". In the previous chapter, you learned the details of what these data types entail, but below are some examples to refresh your memory.

Data Type	Example
Int (Must be a whole number, positive or negative with no decimals, no length restrictions)	*363 or 3.214*
Float (Floating point number must be a positive or negative number with one or more decimals; maybe scientific number an "e" to specify an exponential power of 10)	*29e3*

Complex (Must be written with a "j" as an imaginary character)	*92j*

EXERCISE – Create variable "a" with data value as "3.24", variable "b" with data value as "9e3" and variable "c" with data value as "-39j".

USE YOUR DISCRETION HERE AND WRITE YOUR CODE FIRST

Now, check your code against the correct code below:

a = 3.24   # int

b = 9e3   # float

c = -39j   # complex

print (type (a))

print (type (b))

print (type (c))

Note – The # comments are not required for the correct code and are only mentioned to bolster your understanding of the concept.

Converting one numeric data type to another

As all Python variables are dynamic in nature, you will be able to convert the data type of these variables if needed by deriving a new variable from the variable that you would like to assign a new data type.

Let's continue building on the exercise discussed above.

```
a = 3.24     # int
b = 9e3      # float
c = -39j     # complex

#conversion from int to float
x = float (a)

#conversion from float to complex
y = complex (b)

#conversion from complex to int
z = float (c)
#conversion from int to complex
x1 = int (a)

print (x)
print (y)
print (z)
print (x1)

print (type (x))
print (type (y))
print (type (z))
print (type (x1))
```

EXERCISE – View a random number between 14 and 24 by importing the random module.

USE YOUR DISCRETION HERE AND WRITE YOUR CODE FIRST*

Now, check your code against the correct code below:

import random

print (random.randrange (14, 24))

Variable Casting with Constructor Functions

In the discussion and exercise above, you learned that variables could be declared by simply assigning desired data value to them, and thereby, the variables will assume the pertinent data type based on the data value. However, Python allows you to specify the data types for variables by using classes or "constructor functions" to define the data type for variables. This process is called "Casting".

Here are the 3 constructor functions used for "casting" numeric data type to a variable.

Constructor Functions	Data Type
int ()	Will construct an integer number from an integer literal, a string literal (provided the string is representing a whole number) or a float literal (by rounding down to the preceding whole number)
float ()	Will construct a float number from a

	string literal (provided the string is representing a float or an integer), a float literal or an integer literal
complex ()	Will construct a string from a large number of data types, such as integer literals, float literals, and strings

Here are some examples:

Integer:
a = int (6) # a takes the value 6
b = int (4.6)   # b takes the value 4
c = int ('7')# c takes the value 7

Float:
a = float (6)   # a takes the value 6.0
b = float (4.6)   # b takes the value 4.6
c = float ('7')   # c takes the value 7.0

String:
a = str ('serial')   # a takes the value 'serial'
b = str (4.6)   # b takes the value '4.6'
c = str ('7')   # c takes the value '7.0'

Python Strings

In Python, string data type for a variable is denoted by using single, double, or triple quotation marks. This implies that you can assign string data value to variable by quoting the string of characters. For example, "welcome" is the same as 'welcome' and "'welcome'".

EXERCISE – Create a variable "v" with a string data value as "outfit is cyan" and display it.

USE YOUR DISCRETION HERE AND WRITE YOUR CODE FIRST

Now, check your code against the correct code below:
v = 'outfit is cyan'
print (v)

OUTPUT – outfit is cyan

EXERCISE – Create a variable "A" with a multiple-line string data value as "Looking at the sky tonight, thinking of you by my side! Let the world go on and on; it will be alright if I stay strong!" and display it.
USE YOUR DISCRETION HERE AND WRITE YOUR CODE FIRST

Now, check your code against the correct code below:
a = '''Loving another is never easy,
People tell you it won't be breezy!
You make your own decision,
Don't let the fear stop you from your persuasion!'''
print (a)

OUTPUT – Loving another is never easy,

People tell you it won't be breezy!

You make your own decision,

Don't let the fear stop you from your persuasion!'''

Note – You must use triple quote to create multiline string data values.

String Arrays

In Python, string data values are arrays of bytes that represent Unicode characters as true for most programming languages. But unlike other programming languages, Python lacks data type for individual characters, which are denoted as string data type with length of 1.

The first character of every string is given the position of '0', and subsequently, the subsequent characters will have the position as 1, 2, 3, and so on. In order to display desired characters from a string data value, you can use the position of the character enclosed in square brackets. For example, if you wanted to display the fifth character of the string data value "apple" of variable "x". You will use the command "print (x [4])"

EXERCISE – Create a variable "P" with a string data value as "brilliant" and display the fourth character of this string.

USE YOUR DISCRETION HERE AND WRITE YOUR CODE FIRST

Now, check your code against the correct code below:

P = 'brilliant'

print (P [4])

OUTPUT – l

Slicing

If you would like to view a range of characters, you can do so by specifying the start and the end index of the desired positions and separating the indexes by a colon. For example, to view characters of a string from position 1 to position 3, your code will be *"print (variable [1:3])"*.

You can even view the characters starting from the end of the string by using "negative indexes" and start slicing the string from the end of the string. For example, to view characters of a string from position 4 to position 1, your code will be *"print (variable [-4 : -2])"*.

In order to view the length of the string, you can use the "len ()" function. For example, to view the length of a string, your code will be *"print (len (variable))"*.

EXERCISE – Create a variable "P" with a string data value as "strive for success!" and display characters from position 3 to 6 of this string.

USE YOUR DISCRETION HERE AND WRITE YOUR CODE FIRST

Now, check your code against the correct code below:

P = 'strive for success!'

print (P [4 : 7])

OUTPUT – vef

EXERCISE – Create a variable "x" with a string data value as "coding is cool" and display characters from position 6 to 1, starting the count from the end of this string.

USE YOUR DISCRETION HERE AND WRITE YOUR CODE FIRST

Now, check your code against the correct code below:

x = 'coding is cool'

print (x [-6 : -2])

OUTPUT - isco

EXERCISE – Create a variable "z" with a string data value as "programming champ" and display the length of this string.

USE YOUR DISCRETION HERE AND WRITE YOUR CODE FIRST

Now, check your code against the correct code below:

z = 'programming champ'

print (len (z))

String Methods

There are various built-in methods in Python that can be applied to string data values. Here are the Python codes for some of the most frequently used string methods, using variable "P = 'roses are red!'".

"strip ()" method – To remove any blank spaces at the start and the end of the string.

P = "   roses are red!   "
print (P.strip ())

OUTPUT – roses are red!

"lower ()" method – To result in all the characters of a string in lower case.

P = "ROSES are RED!"
print (P.lower ())
OUTPUT – roses are red!

"upper ()" method – To result in all the characters of a string in upper case.

P = "Roses are Red!"
print (P.upper ())

OUTPUT – ROSES ARE RED!

"replace ()" method – To replace select characters of a string.

P = "roses are red!"
print (P.replace ("roses", "apples"))

OUTPUT – apples are red!

"split ()" method – To split a string into substrings using comma as the separator.

P = "Roses, Apples"
print (P.split ("",))

OUTPUT – ['Roses',   'Apples']

String Concatenation

There might be instances when you need to collate different string variables. This can be accomplished with the use of the "+" logical operator. Here's the syntax for this Python code:

X = "string1"
Y = "string2"
Z = X + Y
print (Z)

Similarly, below is the syntax to insert a blank space between two different string variables.

X = "string1"

41

```
Y = "string2"
Z = X + " " + Y
print (Z)
```

However, Python does not permit the concatenation of string variables with numeric variables. But can be accomplished with the use of the *"format ()"* method, which will format the executed arguments and place them in the string where the placeholders "{ }" are used. Here's the syntax for this Python code:

```
X = numeric
Y = "String"
print (Y. format (X))
```

EXERCISE – Create two variables "A" and "B" with string data values as "Let's have" and "some pizza!" and display them as a concatenated string.

USE YOUR DISCRETION HERE AND WRITE YOUR CODE FIRST

Now, check your code against the correct code below:
```
A = "Let's have"
B = "some pizza!"
C = A + B
print (C)
```

OUTPUT – Let's have some pizza!

EXERCISE – Create two variables "A" with string data values as "her lucky number is" and "B" with numeric data value as "18" and display them as a concatenated string.

USE YOUR DISCRETION HERE AND WRITE YOUR CODE FIRST

Now, check your code against the correct code below:

A = "her lucky number is"

B = "18"

print (A. format (B))

OUTPUT – her lucky number is 18

Python Booleans

In the process of developing a software program, there is often a need to confirm and verify whether an expression is true or false. This is where Python Boolean data type and data values are used. In Python, comparison and evaluation of two data values will result in one of the two Boolean values: "True" or "False".

Here are some examples of comparison statement of numeric data leading to Boolean value:

print (100 > 90)

OUTPUT – True

print (100 == 90)

OUTPUT – False

print (100 < 90)

OUTPUT – False

Let's look at the *"bool ()"* function now, which allows for the evaluation of numeric data as well as string data resulting in "True" or "False" Boolean values.

print (bool (99))

OUTPUT - True

print (bool ("Welcome"))

OUTPUT - True

Here are some key points to remember for Booleans:
1.   If a statement has some kind of content, it would be evaluated as "True".
2.   All string data values will be resulting as "True" unless the string is empty.
3.   All numeric values will be resulting as "True" except "0"
4.   Lists, Tuples, Set, and Dictionaries will be resulting as "True" unless they are empty.
5.   Mostly empty values like (), [], {}, "", False, None and 0 will be resulting as "False".

6. Any object created with the "_len_" function that result in the data value as "0" or "False" will be evaluated as "False".

In Python there are various built-in functions function that can be evaluated as Boolean, for example, the "isinstance()" function, which allows you to determine the data type of an object. Therefore, in order to check if an object is integer, the code will be as below:

X = 123

print (isinstance (X, int))

EXERCISE – Create two variables "X" with string data values as "Just do it!" and "Y" with numeric data value as "3.24" and evaluate them.

USE YOUR DISCRETION HERE AND WRITE YOUR CODE FIRST

Now, check your code against the correct code below:

X = "Just do it!"

Y = 3.24

print (bool (X))

print (bool (Y))

OUTPUT –

True

True

Python Lists

In Python, lists are collections of data types that can be changed, organized, and include duplicate values. Lists are written within square brackets, as shown in the syntax below.

X = ["string001", "string002", "string003"]
print (X)

The same concept of position applies to Lists as the string data type, which dictates that the first string is considered to be at position 0. Subsequently, the strings that will follow are given positions 1, 2, and so on. You can selectively display desired string from a List by referencing the position of that string inside square bracket in the print command, as shown below.

X = ["string001", "string002", "string003"]
print (X [2])

OUTPUT – [string003]

Similarly, the concept of **negative indexing** is also applied to Python List. Let's look at the example below:

X = ["string001", "string002", "string003"]
print (X [-2])

OUTPUT – [string002]

You will also be able to specify a **range of indexes** by indicating the start and end of a range. The result in values of such command on a Python List would be a new List containing only the indicated items. Here is an example for your reference.

X = ["string001", "string002", "string003", "string004", "string005", "string006"]

print (X [2 : 4])

OUTPUT – ["string003", "string004"]

* Remember the first item is at position 0, and the final position of the range (4) is not included.

Now, if you do not indicate the start of this range, it will default to the position 0 as shown in the example below:

X = ["string001", "string002", "string003", "string004", "string005", "string006"]

print (X [: 3])

OUTPUT – ["string001", "string002", "string003"]

Similarly, if you do not indicate the end of this range it will display all the items of the List from the indicated start range to the end of the List, as shown in the example below:

X = ["string001", "string002", "string003", "string004", "string005", "string006"]

print (X [3 :])

OUTPUT – ["string004", "string005", "string006"]

You can also specify a **range of negative indexes** to Python Lists, as shown in the example below:

X = ["string001", "string002", "string003", "string004", "string005", "string006"]

print (X [-3 : -1])

OUTPUT – ["string004", "string005"]

* Remember the last item is at position -1, and the final position of this range (-1) is not included in the Output.

There might be instances when you need to **change the data value** for a Python List. This can be accomplished by referring to the index number of that item and declaring the new value. Let's look at the example below:

X = ["string001", "string002", "string003", "string004", "string005", "string006"]

X [3] = "newstring"

print (X)

OUTPUT – ["string001", "string002", "string003", "newstring", "string005", "string006"]

You can also determine the **length** of a Python List using the "len()" function, as shown in the example below:

X = ["string001", "string002", "string003", "string004", "string005", "string006"] print (len (X))

OUTPUT – 6

Python Lists can also be changed by **adding new items** to an existing list using the built-in "append ()" method, as shown in the example below:

X = ["string001", "string002", "string003", "string004"]

X.append ("newstring")

print (X)

OUTPUT – ["string001", "string002", "string003", "string004", "newstring"]

You can also, add a new item to an existing Python List at a specific position using the built-in "insert ()" method, as shown in the example below:

X = ["string001", "string002", "string003", "string004"]

X.insert (2, "newstring")

print (X)

OUTPUT – ["string001", "string002", "newstring", "string004"]

There might be instances when you need to **copy** an existing Python List. This can be accomplished by using the built-in "copy ( )" method or the "list ( )" method, as shown in the example below:

X = ["string001", "string002", "string003", "string004", "string005", "string006"]

Y = X.copy( )

print (Y)

OUTPUT – ["string001", "string002", "string003", "string004", "string005", "string006"]

X = ["string001", "string002", "string003", "string004", "string005", "string006"]
Y = list (X)
print (Y)

OUTPUT – ["string001", "string002", "string003", "string004", "string005", "string006"]

There are multiple built-in methods to **delete items** from a Python List.

- To selectively delete a specific item, the "remove ()" method can be used.

X = ["string001", "string002", "string003", "string004"]
X.remove ("string002")
print (X)
OUTPUT - ["string001", "string003", "string004"]

- To delete a specific item from the List, the "pop ()" method can be used with the position of the value. If no index has been indicated, the last item of the index will be removed.

X = ["string001", "string002", "string003", "string004"]
X.pop ( )
print (X)

OUTPUT - ["string001", "string002", "string003"]

- To delete a specific index from the List, the "del ()" method can be used, followed by the index within square brackets.

X = ["string001", "string002", "string003", "string004"]
del X [2]
print (X)

OUTPUT - ["string001", "string002", "string004"]

- To delete the entire List variable, the "del ()" method can be used, as shown below.

X = ["string001", "string002", "string003", "string004"]
del X

OUTPUT - .....

- To delete all the string values from the List without deleting the variable itself, the "clear ()" method can be used, as shown below.

X = ["string001", "string002", "string003", "string004"]
X.clear()
print (X)

OUTPUT – [ ]

Concatenation of Lists

You can join multiple lists with the use of the "+" logical operator or by adding all the items from one list to another using the "append ( )" method. The "extend ( )" method can be used to add a list at the end of another list. Let's look at the examples below to understand these commands.

X = ["string001", "string002", "string003", "string004"]
Y = [10, 20, 30, 40]
Z = X + Y
print (Z)

OUTPUT – ["string001", "string002", "string003", "string004", 10, 20, 30, 40]

X = ["string001", "string002", "string003", "string004"]
Y = [10, 20, 30, 40]

For x in Y:
X.append (x)

print (X)

OUTPUT – ["string001", "string002", "string003", "string004", 10, 20, 30, 40]
X = ["string001", "string002", "string003"]
Y = [10, 20, 30]

X.extend (Y)

print (X)

OUTPUT – ["string001", "string002", "string003", 10, 20, 30]

EXERCISE – Create a list "A" with string data values as "red, olive, cyan, lilac, mustard" and display the item at -2 position.

USE YOUR DISCRETION HERE AND WRITE YOUR CODE FIRST

Now, check your code against the correct code below:
A = ["red", "olive", "cyan", "lilac", "mustard"]
print (A [-2])

OUTPUT – ["lilac"]

EXERCISE – Create a list "A" with string data values as "red, olive, cyan, lilac, mustard" and display the items ranging from the string on the second position to the end of the string.

USE YOUR DISCRETION HERE AND WRITE YOUR CODE FIRST

Now, check your code against the correct code below:
A = ["red", "olive", "cyan", "lilac", "mustard"]
print (A [2 :])
OUTPUT – ["cyan", "lilac", "mustard"]

EXERCISE – Create a list "A" with string data values as "red, olive, cyan, lilac, mustard" and replace the string "olive" to "teal".

USE YOUR DISCRETION HERE AND WRITE YOUR CODE FIRST*

Now, check your code against the correct code below:

A = ["red", "olive", "cyan", "lilac", "mustard"]

A [1] = ["teal"]

print (A)

OUTPUT – ["red", "teal", "cyan", "lilac", "mustard"]

EXERCISE – Create a list "A" with string data values as "red, olive, cyan, lilac, mustard" and copy the list "A" to create list "B".

USE YOUR DISCRETION HERE AND WRITE YOUR CODE FIRST

Now, check your code against the correct code below:

A = ["red", "olive", "cyan", "lilac", "mustard"]

B = A.copy ( )

print (B)

OUTPUT – ["red", "olive", "cyan", "lilac", "mustard"]

EXERCISE – Create a list "A" with string data values as "red, olive, cyan, lilac, mustard" and delete the strings "red" and "lilac".

*** USE YOUR DISCRETION HERE AND WRITE YOUR CODE FIRST ***

Now, check your code against the correct code below:
A = ["red", "olive", "cyan", "lilac", "mustard"]
del.A [0, 2]
print (A)

OUTPUT – ["olive", "cyan", "mustard"]

Python Tuples

In Python, Tuples are collections of data types that cannot be changed but can be arranged in specific order. Tuples allow for duplicate items and are written within round brackets, as shown in the syntax below.

Tuple = ("string001", "string002", "string003")
print (Tuple)

Similar to the Python List, you can selectively display the desired string from a Tuple by referencing the position of that string inside square bracket in the print command as shown below.

Tuple = ("string001", "string002", "string003")
print (Tuple [1])

OUTPUT – ("string002")

The concept of **negative indexing** can also be applied to Python Tuple, as shown in the example below:

Tuple = ("string001", "string002", "string003", "string004", "string005")

print (Tuple [-2])

OUTPUT – ("string004")

You will also be able to specify a **range of indexes** by indicating the start and end of a range. The result in values of such command on a Python Tuple would be a new Tuple containing only the indicated items, as shown in the example below:

Tuple = ("string001", "string002", "string003", "string004", "string005", "string006")

print (Tuple [1:5])

OUTPUT – *("string002", "string003", "string004", "string005")*

* Remember the first item is at position 0 and the final position of the range, which is the fifth position in this example, is not included.

You can also specify a **range of negative indexes** to Python Tuples, as shown in the example below:

Tuple = ("string001", "string002", "string003", "string004", "string005", "string006")

print (Tuple [-4: -2])

OUTPUT – *("string004", "string005")*

* Remember the last item is at position -1 and the final position of this range, which is the negative fourth position in this example is not included in the Output.

Unlike Python lists, you cannot directly **change the data value of Python Tuples** after they have been created. However, conversion of a Tuple into a List and then modifying the data value of that List will allow you to subsequently create a Tuple from that updated List. Let's look at the example below:

Tuple1 = ("string001", "string002", "string003", "string004", "string005", "string006")

List1 = list (Tuple1)

List1 [2] = "update this list to create new tuple"

Tuple1 = tuple (List1)

print (Tuple1)

OUTPUT – ("string001", "string002", "update this list to create new tuple", "string004", "string005", "string006")

You can also determine the **length** of a Python Tuple using the "len()" function, as shown in the example below:

Tuple = ("string001", "string002", "string003", "string004", "string005", "string006")

print (len (Tuple))

OUTPUT – 6

You cannot selectively delete items from a Tuple, but you can use the "del" keyword to **delete the Tuple** in its entirety, as shown in the example below:

Tuple = ("string001", "string002", "string003", "string004")
del Tuple

print (Tuple)

OUTPUT – name 'Tuple' is not defined

You can **join multiple Tuples** with the use of the "+" logical operator.

Tuple1 = ("string001", "string002", "string003", "string004")
Tuple2 = (100, 200, 300)

Tuple3 = Tuple1 + Tuple2
print (Tuple3)

OUTPUT – ("string001", "string002", "string003", "string004", 100, 200, 300)

You can also use the "tuple ( )" constructor to create a Tuple, as shown in the example below:

Tuple1 = tuple (("string001", "string002", "string003", "string004"))
print (Tuple1)

EXERCISE – Create a Tuple "X" with string data values as "pies, cake, bread, scone, cookies" and display the item at -3 position.

USE YOUR DISCRETION HERE AND WRITE YOUR CODE FIRST

Now, check your code against the correct code below:
X = ("pies", "cake", "bread", "scone", "cookies")
print (X [-3])

OUTPUT – ("bread")

EXERCISE – Create a Tuple "X" with string data values as "pies, cake, bread, scone, cookies" and display items ranging from -2 to -4.

USE YOUR DISCRETION HERE AND WRITE YOUR CODE FIRST

Now, check your code against the correct code below:
X = ("pies", "cake", "bread", "scone", "cookies")
print (X [-4 : -2])

OUTPUT – ("cake", "bread")

EXERCISE – Create a Tuple "X" with string data values as "pies, cake, bread, scone, cookies" and change its item from "cookies" to "tart" using List function.

Now, check your code against the correct code below:

X = ("pies", "cake", "bread", "scone", "cookies")

Y = list (X)

Y [4] = "tart"

X = tuple (Y)

print (X)

OUTPUT – ("pies", "cake", "bread", "scone", "tart")

EXERCISE – Create a Tuple "X" with string data values as "pies, cake, cookies" and another Tuple "Y" with numeric data values as (2, 12, 22), then join them together.

Now, check your code against the correct code below:

X = ("pies", "cake", "cookies")

Y = (2, 12, 22)

Z = X + Y

print (Z)

OUTPUT – ("pies", "cake", "cookies", 2, 12, 22)

Python Sets

In Python, Sets are collections of data types that cannot be organized and indexed. Sets do not allow for duplicate items and must be written within curly brackets, as shown in the syntax below:

set = {"string1", "string2", "string3"}

print (set)

Unlike the Python List and Tuple, you cannot selectively display desired items from a Set by referencing the position of that item because the Python Set are not arranged in any order. Therefore, items do not have any indexing. However, the "for" loop can be used on Sets (more on this topic later in this chapter).

Unlike Python Lists, you cannot directly **change the data values of Python Sets** after they have been created. However, you can use the "add ()" method to add a single item to Set and use the "update ( )" method to one or more items to an already existing Set. Let's look at the example below:

set = {"string1", "string2", "string3"}

set. add ("newstring")

print (set)

OUTPUT – {"string1", "string2", "string3", "newstring"}

set = {"string1", "string2", "string3"}

set. update (["newstring1", "newstring2", "newstring3",)

print (set)

OUTPUT – {"string1", "string2", "string3", "newstring1", "newstring2", "newstring3"}

You can also determine the **length** of a Python Set using the "len()" function, as shown in the example below:

set = {"string1", "string2", "string3", "string4", "string5", "string6", "string7"}

print (len(set))

OUTPUT – 7

To selectively **delete a specific item from a Set**, the "remove ()" method can be used as shown in the code below:

set = {"string1", "string2", "string3", "string4", "string5"}

set. remove ("string4")

print (set)

OUTPUT – {"string1", "string2", "string3", "string5"}

You can also use the "discard ( )" method to delete specific items from a Set, as shown in the example below:

set = {"string1", "string2", "string3", "string4", "string5"}

set. discard ("string3")

print (set)

OUTPUT – {"string1", "string2", "string4", "string5"}

The "pop ( )" method can be used to selectively delete only the last item of a Set. It must be noted here that since the Python Sets are unordered, any item that the system deems as the last item will be removed. As a result, the output of this method will be the item that has been removed.

```
set = {"string1", "string2", "string3", "string4", "string5"}
A = set.pop ( )
print (A)
print (set)
```

OUTPUT –
String2
{"string1", "string3", "string4", "string5"}

To delete the entire Set, the "del" keyword can be used, as shown below.

```
set = {"string1", "string2", "string3", "string4", "string5"}
delete set
print (set)
```

OUTPUT – name 'set' is not defined

To delete all the items from the Set without deleting the variable itself, the "clear ()" method can be used, as shown below:

```
set = {"string1", "string2", "string3", "string4", "string5"}
set.clear ( )
print (set)
```

OUTPUT – set ( )

You can **join multiple Sets** with the use of the "union ( )" method. The output of this method will be a new set that contains all items from both the sets. You can also use the "update ( )" method to insert all the items from one set into another without creating a new Set.

Set1 = {"string1", "string2", "string3", "string4", "string5"}
Set2 = {15, 25, 35, 45, 55}
Set3 = Set1.union (Set2)
print (Set3)

OUTPUT – {"string1", 15, "string2", 25, "string3", 35, "string4", 45, "string5", 55}

Set1 = {"string1", "string2", "string3", "string4", "string5"}
Set2 = {15, 25, 35, 45, 55}
Set1.update (Set2)
print (Set1)

OUTPUT – {25, "string1", 15, "string4",55, "string2", 35, "string3", 45, "string5"}

You can also use the "set ( )" constructor to create a Set, as shown in the example below:
Set1 = set (("string1", "string2", "string3", "string4", "string5"))
print (Set1)

OUTPUT – {"string3", "string5", "string2", "string4", "string1"}

EXERCISE – Create a Set "Veg" with string data values as "pies, cake, bread, scone, cookies" and add new items "tart", "custard" and "waffles" to this Set.

USE YOUR DISCRETION HERE AND WRITE YOUR CODE FIRST

Now, check your code against the correct code below:
Veg = {"pies", "cake", "bread", "scone", "cookies"}
Veg.update (["tart", "custard", "waffles"])
print (Veg)

OUTPUT – {"pies", "custard", "scone", "cake", "bread", "waffles", "cookies", "tart"}

EXERCISE – Create a Set "Veg" with string data values as "pies, cake, bread, scone, cookies", then delete the last item from this Set.

USE YOUR DISCRETION HERE AND WRITE YOUR CODE FIRST

Now, check your code against the correct code below:
Veg = {"pies", "cake", "bread", "scone", "cookies"}
X = Veg.pop ( )
print (X)
print (Veg)

OUTPUT –
bread

{"pies", "scone", "cake", "cookies"}

EXERCISE – Create a Set "Veg" with string data values as "pies, cake, bread, scone, cookies" and another Set "Veg2" with items as "tart, eggos, custard, waffles". Then combine both these Sets to create a third new Set.

USE YOUR DISCRETION HERE AND WRITE YOUR CODE FIRST

Now, check your code against the correct code below:
Veg = {"pies", "cake", "bread", "scone", "cookies"}
Veg2 = {"tart", "eggos", "custard", "waffles"}

AllVeg = Veg.union (Veg2)   #this Set name may vary as it has not been defined in the exercise

print (AllVeg)

OUTPUT – {"pies", "custard", "scone", "cake", "eggos", "bread", "waffles", "cookies", "tart"}

Python Dictionary

In Python, Dictionaries are collections of data types that can be changed and indexed but are not arranged in any order. Each item in a Python Dictionary will comprise a key and its value. Dictionaries do not allow for duplicate items and must be written within curly brackets, as shown in the syntax below:
dict = {

```
"key01": "value01",
"key02": "value02",
"key03": "value03",
}
print (dict)
```

You can selectively display desired item value from a Dictionary by referencing its key inside square brackets in the print command as shown below:

```
dict = {
"key01": "value01",
"key02": "value02",
"key03": "value03",
}

X = dict ["key02"]
print (X)
```

OUTPUT – value02

You can also use the "get ( )" method to view the value of a key, as shown in the example below:

```
dict = {
"key01": "value01",
"key02": "value02",
"key03": "value03",
}

X = dict.get ("key01")
```

print (X)

OUTPUT – value01

There might be instances when you need to **change the value** of a key in a Python Dictionary. This can be accomplished by referring to the key of that item and declaring the new value. Let's look at the example below:

dict = {
"key01": "value01",
"key02": "value02",
"key03": "value03",
}

dict ["key03"] = "NEWvalue"
print (dict)

OUTPUT – {"key01": "value01", "key02": "value02", "key03": "NEWvalue"}

You can also determine the **length** of a Python Dictionary using the "len()" function, as shown in the example below:

dict = {
"key01": "value01",
"key02": "value02",
"key03": "value03",
"key04": "value04",
"key05": "value05"
}

print (len (dict))

OUTPUT – 5

Python Dictionary can also be changed by **adding** new index key and assigning a new value to that key, as shown in the example below:

dict = {
"key01": "value01",
"key02": "value02",
"key03": "value03",
}

dict ["NEWkey"] = "NEWvalue"
print (dict)

OUTPUT – {"key01": "value01", "key02": "value02", "key03": "value03", "NEWkey": "NEWvalue"}

There are multiple built-in methods to **delete items** from a Python Dictionary.

- To selectively delete a specific item value, the "pop ()" method can be used with the indicated key name.

dict = {
"key01": "value01",
"key02": "value02",
"key03": "value03",

```
}
dict.pop ("key01")
print (dict)
```

OUTPUT – { "key02": "value02", "key03": "value03"}

- To selectively delete the item value that was last inserted, the "popitem ()" method can be used with the indicated key name.

```
dict = {
"key01": "value01",
"key02": "value02",
"key03": "value03",
}
dict.popitem ( )
print (dict)
```

OUTPUT – { "key01": "value01", "key02": "value02"}

- To selectively delete a specific item value, the "del" keyword can also be used with the indicated key name.

```
dict = {
"key01": "value01",
"key02": "value02",
"key03": "value03",
}
del dict ("key03")
```

print (dict)

OUTPUT – { "key01": "value01", "key02": "value02"}

- To delete a Python Dictionary in its entirety, the "del" keyword can also be used as shown in the example below:

dict = {

"key01": "value01",

"key02": "value02",

"key03": "value03",

}

del dict

print (dict)

OUTPUT – name 'dict' is not defined

- To delete all the items from the Dictionary without deleting the Dictionary itself, the "clear ()" method can be used as shown below:

dict = {

"key01": "value01",

"key02": "value02",

"key03": "value03",

}

dict.clear ( )

print (dict)

OUTPUT – { }

There might be instances when you need to **copy** an existing Python Dictionary. This can be accomplished by using the built-in "copy ( )" method or the "dict ( )" method, as shown in the examples below:

dict = {

"key01": "value01",

"key02": "value02",

"key03": "value03",

}

newdict = dict.copy ( )

print (newdict)

OUTPUT – {"key01": "value01", "key02": "value02", "key03": "value03"}

Olddict = {

"key01": "value01",

"key02": "value02",

"key03": "value03",

}

newdict = dict (Olddict)

print (newdict)

OUTPUT – {"key01": "value01", "key02": "value02", "key03": "value03"}

There is a unique feature that supports multiple Python Dictionaries to be **nested** within another Python Dictionary. You can either create a Dictionary containing child Dictionaries, as shown in the example below:

```
WendysFamilyDict = {
"burger1" : {
"name" : "Hamburger",
"price" : 2.99
},
"burger2" : {
"name" : "Cheeseburger",
"price" : 5
},
"burger3" : {
"name" : "Bigburger",
"price" : 1.99
}
}
print (WendysFamilyDict)
```

OUTPUT - {"burger1" : { "name" : "Hamburger", "price" : 2.99}, "burger2" : {"name" : "Cheeseburger", "price" : 5}, "burger3" : {"name" : "Bigburger", "price" : 1.99}}

Or you can create a brand new Dictionary that contain other Dictionaries already existing on the system; your code will look like the one below:

```
burgerDict1 : {
"name" : "Hamburger",
"price" : 2.99
}

burgerDict2 : {
```

"name" : "Cheeseburger",

"price" : 5

}

burgerDict3 : {

"name" : "Bigburger",

"price" : 1.99

}

WendysFamilyDict = {

"burgerDict1" : burgerDict1,

"burgerDict2" : burgerDict2,

"burgerDict3" : burgerDict3

}

print (WendysFamilyDict)

OUTPUT - {"burger1" : { "name" : "Hamburger", "price" : 2.99}, "burger2" : {"name" : "Cheeseburger", "price" : 5}, "burger3" : {"name" : "Bigburger", "price" : 1.99}}

Lastly, you can use the "dict ( )" function to create a new Python Dictionary. The key differences when you create items for the Dictionary using this function are 1. Round brackets are used instead of the curly brackets. 2. Equal to sign is used instead of the semi-colon. Let's look at the example below:

DictwithFunction = dict (key01 = "value01", key02 = "value02", key03 = "value03")

print (DictwithFunction)

OUTPUT – {"key01": "value01", "key02": "value02", "key03": "value03"}

EXERCISE – Create a Dictionary "Hortons" with items containing keys as "type", "size" and "price" with corresponding values as "cappuccino", "grande" and "4.99". Then add a new item with key as "syrup" and value as "hazelnut".

USE YOUR DISCRETION HERE AND WRITE YOUR CODE FIRST

Now, check your code against the correct code below:
```
Hortons = {
"type" : "cappuccino",
"size" : "grande",
"price" : 4.99
}
Hortons ["syrup"] = "hazelnut"
print (Hortons)
```
OUTPUT – {"type" : "cappuccino", "size" : "grande", "price" : 4.99, "syrup" : "hazelnut"}

EXERCISE – Create a Dictionary "Hortons" with items containing keys as "type", "size", and "price" with corresponding values as "cappuccino", "grande" and "4.99". Then use a function to remove the last added item.

USE YOUR DISCRETION HERE AND WRITE YOUR CODE FIRST

Now, check your code against the correct code below:

```
Hortons = {
"type" : "cappuccino",
"size" : "grande",
"price" : 4.99
}
Hortons.popitem ( )
print (Hortons)
OUTPUT – {"type" : "cappuccino", "size" : "grande"}
```

EXERCISE – Create a Dictionary "Hortons" with nested dictionary as listed below:

Dictionary Name	Key	Value
Coffee01	name	cappuccino
	size	venti
Coffee02	name	frappe
	size	grande
Coffee03	name	macchiato
	size	small

USE YOUR DISCRETION HERE AND WRITE YOUR CODE FIRST

Now, check your code against the correct code below:

```
Hortons = {
"coffee01" : {
"name" : "cappuccino",
"size" : "venti"
},
```

```
"coffee02" : {
"name" : "frappe",
"size" : "grande"
},
"coffee03" : {
"name" : "macchiato",
"size" : "small"
}
}
print (Hortons)
```

OUTPUT - {"coffee01" : { "name" : "cappuccino", "size" : "venti"}, "coffee02" : {"name" : "frappe", "size" : "grande"}, "coffee03" : {"name" : "macchiato", "size" : "small"}}

EXERCISE – Use the "dict ()" function to create a Dictionary "Hortons" with items containing keys as "type", "size" and "price" with corresponding values as "cappuccino", "grande" and "4.99".

USE YOUR DISCRETION HERE AND WRITE YOUR CODE FIRST

Now, check your code against the correct code below:
```
Hortons = dict (type = "cappuccino", size = "grande", price = 4.99}
print (Hortons)
```
OUTPUT – {"type" : "cappuccino", "size" : "grande", "price" : 4.99, "syrup" : "hazelnut"}

Day 4: Advance Python Concepts

Python Conditions and If statement

Python allows the usage of multiple mathematical, logical conditions as listed below:

- Equal to – "a == y"
- Not equal – "a !=y"
- Less than – "a < y"
- Less than, equal to – "a <= y"
- Greater than – "a > y"
- Greater than, equal to – "a >=y"

If Statement

All these conditions can be used within loops and **"if statement"**. The "if" keyword must be used to write these statements, as shown in the syntax below:

```
X = numeric1
Y = numeric2
if X > Y:
        print ("X is greater than Y")
```

The most important thing to remember here is that the indentation or the blank space at the beginning of a line in the code above is critical. Unlike other programming languages that use curly brackets, Python programming is driven by indentation in the process of defining the scope of the code. Therefore, writing the Python code below will result in an error.

```
X = numeric1
```

78

Y = numeric2

if X > Y:

print ("X is greater than Y")   #leads to an error

Else-if Statement

You can use the "elif" keyword to evaluate if the preceding condition is not true, then execute the subsequent condition. Here is the syntax followed by an example to help you understand this concept further:

X = numeric1

Y = numeric2

if X > Y:

    print ("X is greater than Y")

elif X == Y:

    print ("X and Y are equal")

Example:

X = 58

Y = 58

if X > Y:

    print ("X is greater than Y")

elif X == Y:

    print ("X and Y are equal")

OUTPUT - X and Y are equal

Else Statement

You can use the "else" keyword to execute any condition if the preceding conditions are not true. Here is the syntax followed by an example to help you understand this concept further:

X = numeric1

Y = numeric2

if X > Y:

    print ("X is greater than Y")

elif X == Y:

    print ("X and Y are equal")

else:

    print ("Y is greater than X")

Example:

X = 58

Y = 59

if X > Y:

    print ("X is greater than Y")

elif X == Y:

    print ("X and Y are equal")

else:

    print ("Y is greater than X")

OUTPUT - Y is greater than X

Alternatively, you can use the "else" keyword without using the "elif" keyword, as shown in the example below:

X = 69

Y = 96

if X > Y:

print ("X is greater than Y")

else:

print ("X is not greater than Y")

OUTPUT - X is not greater than Y

Single Line If Statement

You could even execute single line statements with "If" clause, as shown in the syntax below:

If x > y: print ("y is greater than x")

Single Line If-Else Statement

You could even execute single line statements with "If - Else" clause, as shown in the syntax below:

x = 10

y = 15

print ("x") If x > y else print ("y")

Single Line If-Else Statement with multiple Else

You will also be able to execute single line statements with "If - Else" clause containing multiple "Else" statements in the same line, as shown in the syntax below:

x = 100

y = 100

print ("x") If x > y else print ("=") if a == b else print ("y")

"And" Keyword

If you are looking to combine multiple conditional statements, you can do so with the use of the "and" keyword, as shown in the example below:

x = 20

y = 18

z = 35

if x > y and z > x :

    print ("All conditions are True")

"Or" Keyword

If you are looking to combine multiple conditional statements, the other way you can do so is with the use of the "or" keyword, as shown in the example below:

x = 20

y = 18

z = 35

if x > y or x > z :

    print ("At least one of the conditions is True")

"Nested If" Statements

You can have multiple "if" statements within an "if" statement, as shown in the example below:

x = 110

if x > 50:

    print ("Greater than 50, ")

if x > 90:

    print ("and greater than 100")

else:

print ("Not greater than 100")

"Pass" statements

In Python, if you ever need to execute "if" statements without any content, you must incorporate a "pass" statement to avoid triggering any error. Here is an example to further your understanding of this concept.

x = 20
y = 55
if y > x
    pass

EXERCISE – Write the code to check if X = 69 is greater than Y = 79, the output should read "X is greater than Y". If the first condition is not true, then check if X is equal to Y, the output should read "X and Y are equal" otherwise the output should read "Y is greater than X".

USE YOUR DISCRETION HERE AND WRITE YOUR CODE FIRST

Now, check your code against the correct code below:

X = 69
Y = 79
if X > Y:
    print ("X is greater than Y")
elif X == Y:
    print ("X and Y are equal")
else:

print ("Y is greater than X")

OUTPUT – "Y is greater than X"

EXERCISE – Write the code to check if x = 69 is greater '50', the output should read "Greater than 50". Then check if x is greater than '60', the output should read "And greater than 60", otherwise the output should read "Not greater than 60".

USE YOUR DISCRETION HERE AND WRITE YOUR CODE FIRST

Now, check your code against the correct code below:
x = 69

if x > 50:
    print ("Greater than 50")
if x > 60:
    print ("And greater than 60")
else:
    print ("Not greater than 60")

OUTPUT –
"Greater than 50"
"And greater than 60"

EXERCISE – Write the code to check if x = 9 is greater than y = 19 as well as if z = 25 is greater than x. The output should read if one or both the conditions are true.

Now, check your code against the correct code below:

```
x = 9
y = 19
z = 25
if x > y and z > x :
    print ("Both the conditions are True")
```

OUTPUT – "Both the conditions are True"

EXERCISE – Write the code to check if x = 45 is less than y = 459 or z = 1459 is less than x. The output should read if one or both the conditions are true.

Now, check your code against the correct code below:

```
x = 45
y = 459
z = 1459
if x < y and z < x :
    print ("At least one of the conditions is True")
```

OUTPUT – "At least one of the conditions is True"

Python "While" Loop

Python allows the usage of one of its standard loop commands i.e. "while" loop for execution of a block of statements, given that the initial condition holds true.

Here is the syntax for "while" loop statements:

```
p = num1
while p < num2:
    print (p)
    p += 1
```

In the syntax above, to prevent the loop from continuing with no end, the variable (p) was limited by setting to an increment. It is a pre-requisite for the "while" loop to index the variable in the statement.

"break" statements

These statements allow exiting from the "while" loop, even if the set condition holds true. In the example below, the variable will exit the loop when it reaches 4:

```
p = 2
while p < 7:
    print (p)
    if p == 4
        break
    p += 2
```

OUTPUT –

2

3

4

"continue" statements

These statements allow the system to stop the execution of the current condition and move to the next iteration of the loop. In the example below, system will continue the execution of the subsequent command if the variable equals 2:

```
p = 1
while p < 5:
    p += 1
    if p == 2:
        continue
    print (p)
```

OUTPUT –

1
3
4
5

(Note - The number 2 is missing from the result above)

"else" statement

The "else" statement allows you to execute a set of code after the "while" condition doesn't hold true any longer. The output in the example below will include a statement that the initial condition is no longer true:

```
p = 1
while p < 5:
    print (p)
    p += 1
```

else:

    print ("p is no longer less than 5")

OUTPUT –

1

2

3

4

p is no longer less than 5

EXERCISE – Write the code to print a series of number if x = 1 is smaller than 7.

USE YOUR DISCRETION HERE AND WRITE YOUR CODE FIRST

Now, check your code against the correct code below:

x = 1

while x < 7:

    print (x)

    x += 1

OUTPUT –

1

2

3

4

5

6

EXERCISE – Write the code to print a series of number if x = 1 is smaller than 6 and exit the loop when x is 3.

USE YOUR DISCRETION HERE AND WRITE YOUR CODE FIRST

Now, check your code against the correct code below:

x = 1
while x < 6:
    print (x)
    if x == 3
      break
    x += 1

OUTPUT –

1

2

3

EXERCISE – Write the code to print a series of number if x = 1 is smaller than 6 and continue to execute the initial condition if x is 3 in a new iteration.

USE YOUR DISCRETION HERE AND WRITE YOUR CODE FIRST

Now, check your code against the correct code below:

x = 1
while x < 6:

```
x += 1
if x == 3:
continue
print (x)
```

OUTPUT –

1

2

4

5

6

(Note – The number 3 is missing, but the initial condition is executed in a new iteration.)

EXERCISE – Write the code to print a series of number if x = 1 is smaller than 4. Once this condition turns false, print "x is no longer less than 4".

USE YOUR DISCRETION HERE AND WRITE YOUR CODE FIRST

Now, check your code against the correct code below:

```
x = 1
while x < 4:
    print (x)
    x = 1
else:
    print ("x is no longer less than 4")
```

OUTPUT –

1

2

3

x is no longer less than 4

Python "For" Loop

Another one of the Python standard loops is "for" loop, which is used to execute iterations over a series such as string, tuple, set, dictionary, list. The "for" keyword in Python functions like an iterator found in object-oriented programming languages. It allows the execution of a block of statements once for every single item of tuple, set, list, and other series.

Let's look at the example below:

veg = ["tart", "scone", "cookies"]
for X in veg:
        print (X)

OUTPUT –
tart
scone
cookies

You will notice that in the code above that the variable was not defined. The "for" loop can be executed without setting an index for the variable in the code.

Loops for String

Python strings constitute a series of characters are iterative in nature. So if you wanted to loop through characters of a string, you could simply use the "for" loop as shown in the example below:

for X in "carrot":

    print (X)

OUTPUT –

c

a

r

r

o

t

"break" statements

If you want to exit the loop prior to its completion, you can use the "break" statements as shown in the example below:

veg = ["tart", "scone", "cookies", "pies", "carrot"]

for X in veg:

    print (X)

    if X == "pies":

    break

OUTPUT –

tart

scone

cookies

pies

In the example below, the print command was executed prior to the "break" statement and directly affected the output:

veg = ["tart", "scone", "cookies", "pies", "carrot"]

for X in veg:

    if X == "pies":

        break

print (X)

OUTPUT –

tart

scone

cookies

"continue" statement

Similar to the "while" loop, the "continue" statements in the "for" loop is used to stop the execution of the current condition and move to the next iteration of the loop. Let's looks at the example below to further understand this concept:

veg = ["tart", "scone", "cookies", "pies", "carrot"]

for X in veg:

    if X == "cookies":

        continue

print (X)

OUTPUT –

tart

scone

pies

carrot

"range" function

The "range ( )" function can be used to loop through a block of code for a specific number of times. This function will result in a series of number beginning with "0" by default, with regular increments of 1 and ending at a specific number.

Here is an example of this function:

for X in range (5):

  print (X)

OUTPUT –

0

1

2

3

4

Note – The "range ( )" function defaulted to 0 as the first output, and the final value of the range, 5, is excluded from the output.

Let's look at another example with a start and end value of the "range ( )" function:

for X in range (1, 5):

  print (X)

OUTPUT –

1

2

3

4

In the example below, we will specify the increment value, which is set to 1 by default:

for X in range (3, 20, 5):

    print (X)

OUTPUT –

3

8

13

18

"Else" in "For" Loop

You can use the "else" keyword to specify a set of code that need to be executed upon the completion of the loop, as shown in the example below:

for X in range (5):

    print (X)

else:

    print ("The loop was completed")

OUTPUT –

0

1

2

3

4

The loop was completed

"Nested" Loops

When loops are defined within a loop, execution of the inner loop will occur once for each iteration of the outer loop. Let's look at the example below, where we want every single adjective must be printed for each listed vegetable:

adjective = ["olive", "leafy", "healthy"]
veg = ["spinach", "kale", "asparagus"]

for X in adjective:
    for Y in veg:
        print (X, Y)

OUTPUT –
olive spinach
olive kale
olive asparagus
leafy spinach
leafy kale
leafy asparagus
healthy spinach
healthy kale
healthy asparagus

"pass" statements

In Python, if you ever need to execute "for" loops without any content, you must incorporate a "pass" statement to avoid triggering any error. Here is an example to further your understanding of this concept.

for X in [1, 2, 3]
    pass

OUTPUT - ......

The empty "for" loop code above would have resulted in an error without the "pass" statement.

EXERCISE – Write the code to loop through a list of colors ("cyan", "lilac", "red") without defining a variable. Then loop through the characters of the string "cyan".

USE YOUR DISCRETION HERE AND WRITE YOUR CODE FIRST

Now, check your code against the correct code below:

colors = ["cyan", "lilac", "red"]

for A in colors:

    print (A)

for B in "cyan":

    print (B)

OUTPUT –

cyan

lilac

red

c

y

a

n

EXERCISE – Write the code to loop through a list of colors ("cyan", "lilac", "red", "white") without defining a variable. Then break the loop at "red", without printing it in the result.

USE YOUR DISCRETION HERE AND WRITE YOUR CODE FIRST

Now, check your code against the correct code below:

colors = ["cyan", "lilac", "red", "white"]

for A in colors:

    if A == "red":

        break

    print (A)

OUTPUT –

cyan

lilac

EXERCISE – Write the code to loop through a range of numbers starting with 5 and ending with 30. Make sure to define the increments at 6.

USE YOUR DISCRETION HERE AND WRITE YOUR CODE FIRST

Now, check your code against the correct code below:

for X in range (5, 30, 6):

    print (X)

OUTPUT –

5

11

16

22

28

EXERCISE – Write the code to loop phones ("iPhone", "Samsung", "Google"), and loop that with colors ("black", "white", "gold") using nested loops.

USE YOUR DISCRETION HERE AND WRITE YOUR CODE FIRST

Now, check your code against the correct code below:

colors = ["black", "white", "gold"]

phones = ["iPhone", "Samsung", "Google"]

for X in colors:

    for Y in phones:

    print (X, Y)

OUTPUT –

black iPhone

black Samsung

black Google

white iPhone

white Samsung

white Google

gold iPhone

gold Samsung

gold Google

Python Classes and Objects

Python is one of the many object oriented coding languages. Every entity of Python can be considered an object and has its own methods and properties. In Python, Classes are used to construct these objects serving as object blueprints.

A Python Class can be created using the keyword "class" with a predefined property (p) as shown in the syntax below:

class ClassName:

   p = 2

A Python Object can then be created from the Python Class created above, as shown in the syntax below:

Object1 = ClassName ( )

print (object1.p)

Built-in Function

In reality, creation of classes and objects is much more complex than the basic syntax provided above. This is where a built-in function to create classes called "__init__()" is used. When the classes are being created, this inherent class function is executed with it. The "__init__()" function is mostly used for assigning values to object properties and other actions that are required for creation of an object. Let's look at the example below to understand this function:

100

```
class Vehicle:
    def __init__ (self, name, year)
    self.name = name
    self.name = year


v1 = Vehicle ("AUDI", 2018)


print (v1.name)
print (v1.year)


OUTPUT - AUDI    2018
```

Object Methods

There are certain methods that can be created with the Python Objects. These methods can be considered as functions of that object. For example, to create a function that would print a comment regarding ownership of the vehicle and executed on the object v1, the command below will be used:

```
class Vehicle:
    def __init__ (self, name, year)
    self.name = name
    self.name = year


def newfunc (ownership):
    print ("I am a proud owner of " + self.name)


v1 = Vehicle ("AUDI", 2018)
v1.newfunc ()
```

OUTPUT – I am a proud owner of AUDI

Reference Parameter

To refer to the latest instance of a class, the "self" parameter is used. It allows you to access variables that have been derived from a class. This parameter can be named as needed and does not have to be named "self". The important thing to remember here is that the first parameter defined for a class will become the reference parameter for that class, as shown in the example below:

class Vehicle:

def __init__ (refobject, name, year)

refobject.name = name

refobject.name = year

def newfunc (xyz):

print ("I am a proud owner of " + xyz.name)

v1 = Vehicle ("AUDI", 2018)

v1.newfunc ()

OUTPUT – I am a proud owner of AUDI

There might be instances when you need to **change the properties** of an object. You can easily do so by declaring the new property of the object as shown in the example below:

class Vehicle:

def __init__ (refobject, name, year)

refobject.name = name

refobject.name = year

```
def newfunc (xyz):
    print ("I am a proud owner of " + xyz.name)


v1 = Vehicle ("AUDI", 2018)
v1.year = 2019
```

You can use the "del" keyword to selectively **remove properties of an object**, as shown in the example below:

```
class Vehicle:
    def __init__ (refobject, name, year)
    refobject.name = name
    refobject.name = year


def newfunc (xyz):
    print ("I am a proud owner of " + xyz.name)


v1 = Vehicle ("AUDI", 2018)


del v1.year


print (v1.age)
```

OUTPUT – 'Vehicle' object has no 'year' attribute

You can also use the "del" keyword to entirely **delete an object**, as shown in the example below:

```
class Vehicle:
    def __init__ (refobject, name, year)
    refobject.name = name
```

refobject.name = year

def newfunc (xyz):
print ("I am a proud owner of " + xyz.name)

v1 = Vehicle ("AUDI", 2018)

del v1

OUTPUT – NameError: 'v1' is not defined

The "pass" statement

The definition of a Python Class must contain values, or you will receive an error. However, there might be instances when the definition of a class does not have any content. In such a case, you can use the "pass" statement to avoid getting an error. Look at the example below:

class Vehicle: # this class definition is empty
pass   # used to avoid any errors

EXERCISE – Create a Class "KafeShop" with properties as "type" and "size" with corresponding values as "cappuccino" and "large", respectively.

USE YOUR DISCRETION HERE AND WRITE YOUR CODE FIRST

Now, check your code against the correct code below:
class KafeShop:

```
def __init__ (refobject, type, size)
    refobject.type = type
    refobject.size = size


c1 = KafeShop ("cappuccino", "large")


print (c1.type)
print (c1.size)
OUTPUT – cappuccino     large
```

EXERCISE – Create a Class "KafeShop" with properties as "type" and "size" with corresponding values as "cappuccino" and "large" respectively. Create a new function "funct1" that would print "I would like to order a" and execute it on the object.

USE YOUR DISCRETION HERE AND WRITE YOUR CODE FIRST

Now, check your code against the correct code below:
```
class KafeShop:
    def __init__ (refobject, type, size)
        refobject.type = type
        refobject.size = size


    def funct1 (refobject):
        print ("I would like to order a" + refobject.type)


c1 = KafeShop ("cappuccino", "large")
c1.funct1 ( )
```

OUTPUT – I would like to order a cappuccino

Python Operators

In Python, a variety of Operators can be used to perform operations on a Python variable and its values. The different groups of Python operators are provided below:

Arithmetic Operators can be utilized with numerical values to execute basic math calculations.

Name	Operator	Sample
Add	+	J + K
Subtract	-	J - K
Multiply	*	J * K
Divide	/	J / K
Modulus	%	J % K
Exponentiation	**	J ** K
Floor division	//	J // K

Assignment Operators can be utilized for the assignment of values to a variable.

Name	Sample
=	J = 5
+=	J += 3
-=	J -= 3
*=	J *= 3

/=	J /= 3
%=	J %= 3
//=	J //= 3
**=	J **= 3
&=	J &= 3
|=	J |= 3
^=	J ^= 3
>>=	J >>= 3
<<=	J <<= 3

Comparison Operators can be utilized to draw a comparison between the values.

Name	Operator	Sample
Equal	==	J == K
Not equal	!=	J != K
Greater than	>	J > K
Less than	<	J < K
Greater than or equal to	>=	J >= K
Less than or equal to	<=	J <= K

Logical Operators can be utilized to generate a combination of conditional statements.

Operator	Usage	Sample
and	Will return "True" if both the	J < 5

	statements hold true.	and J < 10
or	Will return "True" if one of the statements holds true.	J < 5 or J < 4
not	Will reverse the results and return "False" if the results are true.	Not (J < 5 and J < 10)

Identity Operators can be utilized to draw a comparison between two objects to check whether the same object was created more than once using the same memory location.

Operator	Usage	Sample
is	Will return true if the two variables are the same object.	J is K
is not	Will return true if the two variables are not the same object.	J is not K

Membership Operators can be utilized to test if select sequence can be found in an object.

Operator	Usage	Sample
in	Will return True if a sequence with a specific value can be found in the	J in K

	object.	
not in	Will return True if a sequence with a specific value cannot be found in the object.	J not in K

Bitwise Operators can be utilized to draw a comparison between two numeric values.

Operator	Usage	Sample
&	AND	Will set each bit to 1 if the two bits are 1
|	OR	Will set each bit to 1 if one of the two bits is 1
^	XOR	Will set each bit to 1 if only one of the two bits is 1
~	NOT	Will invert all the bits
<<	Zero fill left shift	Shifts left by pushing zero in from the right, making the left most bit to be dropped
>>	Signed right shift	Shifts right by pushing copies of the left most bit in from the left, making the right most bit to be dropped

Day 5: Built-In Functions

Like most programming languages, Python boasts a number of built-in functions to make your life easier while coding a software program. Here is a list of all such built-in functions:

Function	Description
abs ()	Will result in the absolute values of the numbers.
all ()	Will result in True if all items within an iterative object are true.
any ()	Will result in True if any item of the iterative object holds true.
ascii ()	Will result in a readable version of an object and replace non-ascii characters with escape characters.
bin ()	Will result in the binary version of the numbers.
bool ()	Will result in the boolean values of indicated objects.
bytearray ()	Will result in an array of bytes.
bytes ()	Will result in bytes objects.
callable ()	Will result in True if a specific object is callable or else results in False.
chr ()	Will result in a character from the indicated Unicode code.

classmethod ()	Will convert any method into class method.
compile ()	Will result in the indicated source as an object, ready for execution.
complex ()	Will result in a complex number.
delattr ()	Will delete specific attributes (property or method) from the indicated object.
dict ()	Will result in a dictionary.
dir ()	Will result in a list of properties and methods of the specific object.
divmod ()	Will result in the quotient and the remainder when one argument is divided by another.
enumerate ()	Will take a collection and result in enumerate objects.
eval ()	Will evaluate and execute an expression.
exec ()	Will execute the indicated code (or object)
filter ()	Uses a filter function to exclude items in an iterative object.
float ()	Will result in floating point numbers.
format ()	Will format the indicated value.
frozenset ()	Will result in a frozen set object.
getattr ()	Will result in the value of the indicated attribute (property or method).

globals ()	Will result in the most recent global symbol table as a dictionary.
hasattr ()	Will result in True if the indicated object has the indicated attribute.
hash ()	Will result in the hash value of the indicated object.
help ()	Will execute the built-in help system.
hex ()	Conversion of numbers into hexadecimal values.
id ()	Will result in the identity of an object.
input ()	Will allow user input.
int ()	Will result in an integer number.
isinstance ()	Will result in True if the indicated object is an instance of the indicated object.
issubclass ()	Will result in True if the indicated class is a subclass of the indicated object.
iter ()	Will result in an iterative object.
len ()	Will result in the length of an object.
list ()	Will result in a list.
locals ()	Will result in an updated dictionary of the current local symbol table.
map ()	Will result in the indicated iterator with the indicated function applied to each item.
max ()	Will result in the largest item of an iteration.

memoryview ()	Will result in memory view objects.
min ()	Will result in the smallest item of an iteration.
next ()	Will result in the next item in an iteration.
object ()	Will result in a new object.
oct ()	Converts a number into an octet.
open ()	Will open files and result in file objects.
ord ()	Conversion of an integer representing the Unicode of the indicated character.
pow ()	Will result in the value of a to the power of b.
print ()	Will print to the standard output device.
property ()	Will retrieve, set, and delete a property.
range ()	Will result in a sequence of numbers, beginning from 0 and increments of 1.
repr ()	Will result in a readable version of objects.
reversed ()	Will result in a reversed iteration.
round ()	Rounding of a number.
set ()	Will result in new set objects.
setattr ()	Will set attributes of the objects.
slice ()	Will result in a sliced objects.
sorted ()	Will result in sorted lists.
staticmethod	Will convert methods into a static

()	method.
str ()	Will result in string objects.
sum ()	Will sum the items of iterations.
super ()	Will result in an object representing the parent class.
tuple ()	Will result in tuples.
type ()	Will result in the type of objects.
vars ()	Will result in the _dict_ property of objects.
zip ()	Will result in a single iteration from multiple iterations.

Python Built-in String methods

There are a number of built-in Python methods specifically for strings of data, which will result in new values for the string without making any changes to the original string. Here is a list of all such methods.

Method	Description
capitalize ()	Will convert the initial character to upper case.
casefold ()	Will convert strings into lower case.
center ()	Will result in centered strings.
count ()	Will result in the number of times an indicated value appears in a string.
encode ()	Will result in an encoded version of the

	strings.
endswith ()	Will result in true if the string ends with the indicated value.
expandtabs ()	Will set the tab size of the string.
find ()	Will search the string for indicated value and result in its position.
format ()	Will format indicated values of strings.
format_map ()	Will format indicated values of strings.
index ()	Will search the string for indicated value and result in its position.
isalnum ()	Will result in True if all string characters are alphanumeric.
isalpha ()	Will result in True if all string characters are alphabets.
isdecimal ()	Will result in True if all string characters are decimals.
isdigit ()	Will result in True if all string characters are digits.
isidentifier ()	Will result in True if the strings is an identifier.
islower ()	Will result in True if all string characters are lower case.
isnumeric ()	Will result in True if all string characters are numeric.

isprintable ()	Will result in True if all string characters are printable.
isspace ()	Will result in True if all string characters are whitespaces.
istitle ()	Will result in True if the string follows the rules of a title.
isupper ()	Will result in True if all string characters are upper case.
join ()	Will join the elements of an iteration to the end of the string.
ljust ()	Will result in a left-justified version of the string.
lower ()	Will convert a string into lower case.
lstrip ()	Will result in a left trim version of the string.
maketrans ()	Will result in a translation table to be used in translations.
partition ()	Will result in a tuple where the string is separated into 3 sections.
replace ()	Will result in a string where an indicated value is replaced with another indicated value.
rfind ()	Will search the string for an indicated value and result in its last position.
rindex ()	Will search the string for an indicated value and result in its last position.

rjust ()	Will result in the right justified version of the string.
rpartition ()	Will result in a tuple where the string is separated into 3 sections.
rsplit ()	Will split the string at the indicated separator and result in a list.
rstrip ()	Will result in a new string version that has been trimmed at its right.
split ()	Will split the string at the indicated separator and result in a list.
splitlines ()	Will split the string at line breaks and result in a list.
startswith ()	Will result in true if the string starts with the indicated value.
strip ()	Will result in a trimmed version of the string.
swapcase ()	Will swap the alphabet cases.
title ()	Will convert the first character of each word to upper case.
translate ()	Will result in a translated string.
upper ()	Will convert a string into upper case.
zfill ()	Will fill the string with the indicated number of 0 values at the beginning.

Python Random Numbers

A "random ()" function does not exist in Python, but it has an embedded module called "random" that may be utilized to create numbers randomly when needed. For instance, if you wanted to call the "random" module and display a number randomly between 100 and 500, you can accomplish this by executing the code below:

import random

print (random.randrange (100, 500))

OUTPUT – Any number between 100 and 500 will be randomly displayed.

There are a number of defined methods in the random module as listed below:

Method	Description
betavariate ()	Will result in random float numbers between 0 and 1 based on the Beta distribution.
choice ()	Will result in random elements on the basis of the provided sequence.
choices ()	Will result in a list consisting of a random selection from the provided sequence.
expovariate ()	Will result in a float number randomly displayed between 0 and -1, or between 0 and 1 for negative parameters on the

	basis of the statistical exponential distributions.
gammavariate ()	Will result in a float number displayed between 0 and 1 on the basis of the statistical Gamma distribution.
gauss ()	Will result in a float number displayed between 0 and 1 on the basis of the Gaussian distribution, which is widely utilized in probability theory.
getrandbits ()	Will result in a number that represents the random bits.
getstate ()	Will result in the current internal state of the random number generator.
lognormvariate ()	Will result in a float number randomly displayed between 0 and 1 on the basis of a log-normal distribution, which is widely utilized in probability theory.
normalvariate()	Will result in a float number randomly displayed between 0 and 1 on the basis of the normal distribution, which is widely utilized in probability theory.
paretovariate()	Will result in a float number randomly displayed between 0 and 1 on the basis of the Pareto distribution, which is widely utilized in probability theory.
randint ()	Will result in a random number

	between the provided range.
random ()	Will result in a float number randomly displayed between 0 and 1.
randrange ()	Will result in a random number between the provided range.
sample ()	Will result in a sample of the sequences.
seed ()	Will trigger the random number generator.
setstate ()	Will restore the internal state of the random number generator.
shuffle ()	Will take a sequence and result in a sequence but in some random order.
triangular ()	Will result in a random float number between two provided parameters. You could also set a mode parameter for specification of the midpoint between the two other parameters.
uniform ()	Will result in a random float number between two provided parameters.
vonmisesvariat e()	Will result in a float number randomly displayed between 0 and 1 on the basis of the von "Mises distribution", which is utilized in directional statistics.
weibullvariate()	Will result in a float number randomly displayed between 0 and 1 on the basis

	of the Weibull distribution, which is utilized in statistics.

Python Built-in List methods

Python supports a number of built-in methods that can be used on lists or arrays, as listed in the table below:

Method	Description
append ()	Will insert an element at the end of the list.
clear ()	Will remove all the list elements.
copy ()	Will result in a replica of the list.
count ()	Will result in the number of elements with the indicated value.
extend ()	Will add the elements of a list (or any iterator), to the end of the current list.
index ()	Will result in the index of the first element with the indicated value.
insert ()	Will add an element at the indicated position.
pop ()	Will remove the element at the indicated position.
remove ()	Will remove the first item with the indicated value.
reverse ()	Will reverse the order of the list.
sort ()	Will sort the list.

Python Built-in Tuple methods

Python supports a couple of built-in methods that can be used on tuples, as listed in the table below:

Method	Description
count ()	Will result in the number of times an indicated value appears in the tuple.
index ()	Will search a tuple for the indicated value and result in the position of where the value is found.

Python Built-in Set methods

Python also supports a variety of embedded methods that can be used on sets that are listed in the table below:

Method	Description
"add ()"	Will add an element to the set.
"clear ()"	Will remove all the elements from the set.
"copy ()"	Will result in a replica of the set.
"difference ()"	Will result in a set that contains the difference between 2 or more sets.
"difference_update ()"	Will remove the items from a set that can be found in another, indicated set.
"discard ()"	Will remove the indicated item.
"intersection	Will result in a set that is the

()"	intersection of couple other sets.
"intersection_update ()"	Will remove the items from a set that are not present in another indicated set.
"isdisjoint ()"	Will determine if intersection exists between two sets.
"issubset ()"	Will determine if the identified set contains another set.
"issuperset ()"	Will determine if a different set contain the identified set or not.
"pop ()"	Will remove an element from the set.
"remove ()"	Will remove the indicated element.
"symmetric_difference ()"	Will result in a set with the symmetric differences of the two indicated sets.
"symmetric_difference_update ()"	Will insert the symmetric differences from the indicated set and other sets.
"union ()"	Will result in a set containing the union of sets.
"update ()"	Will update the set with the union of the inidcated set and other sets.

Python Built-in Dictionary methods

Python also supports a large number of built-in methods that can be used on dictionaries that are listed in the table below:

Method	Description

clear ()	Will remove all the elements from the dictionary.
copy ()	Will result in a copy of the dictionary.
fromkeys ()	Will result in a dictionary with the indicated keys and values.
get ()	Will result in the values of the indicated key.
items ()	Will result in a list containing a tuple for every key-value pair.
keys ()	Will result in a list containing the keys of the dictionary.
pop ()	Will remove the elements with the indicated key.
popitem ()	Will remove the key value pair that was most recently added.
setdefault ()	Will result in the values of the indicated key. In case the key is not found, a new key will be added with the indicated values.
update ()	Will update the dictionary with the indicated key value pairs.
values ()	Will result in a list of all the values in the dictionary.

Python Built-in File methods

Python also supports a large number of built-in methods that can be used on file objects that are listed in the table below:

Method	Description
close ()	Will close the file
detach ()	Will result in a separate raw stream.
fileno ()	Will result in a number representing the stream, per the operating system processing.
flush ()	Will flush the internal buffer.
isatty ()	Will result in determination if the file stream is interactive.
read ()	Will result in the content of the file.
readable ()	Will result in determination if the file stream is readable or not.
readline ()	Will result in one line from the file.
readlines ()	Will result in a list of lines from the file.
seek ()	Will modify the position of the file.
seekable ()	Will result in determination if the file permits modification of its position.
tell ()	Will result in the current position of the file.
truncate ()	Will change the size of the file to the indicated value.

writeable ()	Will result in determination if the file permits writing over.
write ()	Will write the indicated string to the file.
writelines ()	Will writes a list of strings to the file.

Python Keywords

Python contains some keywords that cannot be used to define a variable or used as a function name or any other unique identifier. These select Python keywords are listed in the table below:

Method	Description
"and"	Logical operator.
"as"	For creating an alias.
"assert"	To debug.
"break"	For breaking out of a loop.
"class"	For defining a class.
"continue"	For continuing to the next iteration of a loop.
"def"	For defining a function.
"del"	For deleting an object.
"elif"	For use in conditional statements, similar to "else if".
"else"	For use in conditional statements.
"except"	For use with exceptions, so the program knows the steps to follow in

	case of an exception.
"FALSE"	One of the data values assigned only to Boolean data type.
"finally"	For use with exceptions, this set of code would be executed regardless of any occurrences of an exception.
"for"	Used in creation of a "for loop".
"from"	For importing particular part of a module.
"global"	For declaring a global variable.
"if"	For making conditional statements.
"import"	For importing desired module.
"in"	For checking a specific data value within a tuple or a list.
"is"	For testing two variables that may be equal.
"lambda"	For creating an anonymous function.
"None"	For representation of null data value.
"nonlocal"	For declaration of a non-local variable.
"not"	Logical operator.
"or"	Logical operator.
"pass"	Will result in a null statement that would not be executed.
"raise"	Used to raise an exception to the statement.

"result in"	Used for exiting a function and resulting in a data value.
"TRUE"	One of the data values assigned only to Boolean data type.
"try"	Used for making "try except" statements.
"while"	For creating a "while loop".
"with"	Used for simplification of the handling procedure for exceptions.
"yield"	For terminating a function and resulting in a generator.

Review Quiz

Answer the questions below to verify your understanding of the concepts explained in this chapter. The answer key can be found at the end of the quiz.

1. Name the built in function that will allow you to output Boolean values of indicated objects.

2. Name the built in function that will allow you to output a list of properties and methods of the specific object.

3. Name the built in function that will allow you to output an updated dictionary of the current local symbol table.

4. Name the built in function that will allow you to defined the attributes of the objects.

5. Name the built in string method that will allow you to convert the initial character to upper case.

6. Name the built in string method that will allow you to search the string for indicated value and result in its position.

7. Name the built in string method that will allow you to join the elements of an iteration to the end of the string.

8. Name the built in string method that will allow you to replace an indicated value of a string into another one.

9. Name the built in random number method that will allow you to output a list consisting of a random selection from the provided sequence.

10. Name the built in random number method that will allow you to output the current internal state of the random number generator.

11. Name the built in random number method that will allow you to output a float number randomly displayed between 0 and 1.

12. Name the built in random number method that will allow you to output a random float number between two provided parameters.

13. Name the built in list method that will allow you to insert an element at the end of the list.

14. Name the built in list method that will allow you to add the elements of a list (or any iterator), to the end of the current list.

15. Name the built in tuple method that will allow you to output the number of times an indicated value appears in the tuple.

16. Name the built in tuple method that will allow you to search a tuple for the indicated value and result in the position of where the value is found.

17. Name the built in Set method that will allow you to remove all the elements from the set.

18. Name the built in Set method that will allow you to output a set that is the intersection of couple other sets.

19. Name the built in Dictionary method that will allow you to output a dictionary with the indicated keys and values.

20. Name the built in Dictionary method that will allow you to remove the key value pair that was most recently added.

Answer Key

1.   bool ( )
2.   dir ( )
3.   locals ( )
4.   setattr ( )
5.   capitalize ( )
6.   find ( )
7.   join ( )
8.   replace ( )
9.   choices ( )
10. getstate ( )
11. random ( )
12. uniform ( )
13. append ( )
14. extend ( )
15. count ( )
16. index ( )
17. clear ( )
18. intersection ( )
19. fromkeys ( )
20. popitem ( )

Day 6: Web Development

Django

According to the Django Software Foundation, "Django is a free and open-source, high-level Python Web framework that encourages rapid development and clean, pragmatic design. Built by experienced developers, it takes care of much of the hassle of Web development, so you can focus on writing your app without needing to reinvent the wheel". The main objective of Django is to facilitate the development of sophisticated websites that are driven by databases. Its name is credited to the famous guitarist "Django Reinhardt" and was developed in late 2003 by computer scientists at the Lawrence Journal World newspaper, Adrian Holovaty, and Simon Willison. In July 2005, this framework was launched under a BSD license and was rolled up to the management of the "Django Software Foundation" in June 2008.

This framework promotes reusability and easy plugging in the component, fewer codes, limited connection, faster development, and the no repetition principle. "Django" extensively uses Python for the development of configuration documents and data models. It can be equipped with an optional administrative interface, which is dynamically developed by introspection and administrative model configurations, to allow creating, reading, updating and deleting files as needed. Several of the widely renowned websites are based on this framework, such as Public Broadcasting Service, Instagram, Mozilla, Washington Times, Disqus, Bitbucket, and Nextdoor.

Although the fundamental framework of Django has its own naming conventions, like naming the objects that can be called and used to generate views of the HTTP responses, it could still be considered a model-template-view (MTV) architectural pattern. It comprises of an object-relational mapper (ORM) that acts as a mediator between data models (Python classes) and a relational database (Model), a system to process HTTP requests using a web template system or View, and a standard expression driven "URL dispatcher" or "Controller".

The underlying framework also contains the features listed below:

- A standalone and light weight webserver to develop and test the websites.
- A system to serialize and validate HTML forms, which is capable of translating between appropriate database storage values and these forms.
- A template system using the principle of inheritance as found in object oriented programming.
- A caching framework, which is capable of using a variety of caching techniques.
- Support for middleware classes, which are capable of intervening and performing custom tasks at different phases of request processing.
- An integrated dispatch system allowing application components to relay occurrences to one another, through pre-defined signals.
- An internationalization system, which includes translations of various components of Django into a multitude of languages.

- A serialization system, which is capable of producing and reading XML and/or JSON representations of the Django model instances
- A system that allows extension of the template engine functionality.
- An interface to the integrated unit test framework of Python.
- "Django REST Framework" constitutes a strong and adaptable "Web API construction" toolkit.

Installing Django

All web applications and/or websites developed using Django contains 3 different layers, namely, model, view and controller pertaining to the database, its appearance and logic respectively. This is also referred to as the "MVC" or model view controller architecture. Now, let's start with the installation of Django on your system by running the Python file below:

"pip install Django == 1.7.2"

Now let's generate the directory "/Django-welcome/" for the application and create a new file called welcome.py using the code below:

```
#!/usr/bin/env python
import sys
from django.conf import settings
from django.conf.urls import patterns
from django.http import HttpResponse
```

```
from django.core.management import execute_from_command_line

settings.configure(
DEBUG = True,
SECRET_KEY = 'asecretkey',
ROOT_URLCONF = sys.modules [__name__],
)

def index(request):
return HttpResponse ('Welcome')

urlpatterns = patterns (' ',
(r'^welcome/$', index),
)

if __name__ == "__main__":
execute_from_command_line (sys.argv)
```

Remember the script you just created can be executed with the command below:

"python welcome.py runserver"

Web application development using Django

In this section we will be creating a web based application to take notes. The first step is creation of the directory "mywebsite" using the Python command below:

"Django-admin startproject mywebsite"

Now, to configure the database as needed, open "mywebsite/mywebsite/settings.py" and execute the code below:

```
"DATABASES = {
'default': {
'ENGINE': 'django.db.backends.sqlite3',
'NAME': os.path.join(BASE_DIR, 'db.sqlite3'),
}
}"
```

You can choose from oracle, mysql, or sqlite3 and give desired name to the database. With SQLite the database is created by default. Browse up a directory to /mywebsite/ and execute the command below:

"python manage.py runserver"

The terminal will display the code below:

"Performing system checks...

System check identified no issues (0 silenced).

You have unapplied migrations; your app may not work properly until they are applied.
Run 'python manage.py migrate' to apply them.

August 16, 2019 - 14:45:29
Django version 1.7.2, using settings 'myapp.settings'

Starting development server at http://127.0.0.1:9000/

Quit the server with CONTROL-C.

[16/Aug/2019 14:45:35] "GET / HTTP/1.1" 200 1759"

If you opened the http in the code above in your web browser, you will see a window similar to the picture shown below:

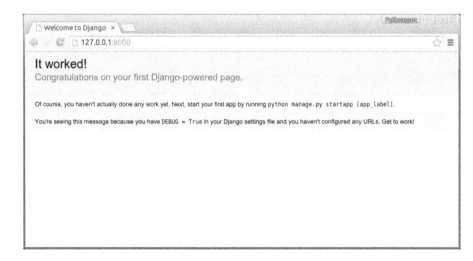

At this point we already have our first project created that is capable of holding multiple applications. So let's create a note taking application by first executing the command below:

"python manage.py startapp notes"

The code above will result in creation of the file below:

"notes/

init.py

admin.py

migrations/

    init.py

models.py

tests.py

views.py"

Step 2 is to update the database model to the command below:

"from django.db import models

class Note (models.Model):

text = models.CharField (max_length=120)

created = models.DateTimeField (auto_now_add=True)"

Step 3 is to open the website settings and add the web application using the command below:

"INSTALLED_APPS = (

'django.contrib.admin',

'django.contrib.auth',

'django.contrib.contenttypes',

'django.contrib.sessions',

'django.contrib.messages',

'django.contrib.staticfiles',

'notes'

)"

Step 4 is to update the database by executing *"python manage.py syncdb"* file and then updating the *"/mywebsite/mywebsite/admin.py"* using the command below:

"from django.contrib import admin

 # Register your models here.
from .models import Note

class NoteAdmin (admin.ModelAdmin):
class Meta:
model = Note

admin.site.register (Note,NoteAdmin)"

Now, you can run the commands below and kickstart the server:
"python manage.py makemigrations notes
python manage.py migrate

manage.py runserver"
As soon as the administration panel is opened up using the defined website address http://127.0.0.1:9000/admin, our browser will appear similar to the picture shown below containing notes administration option:

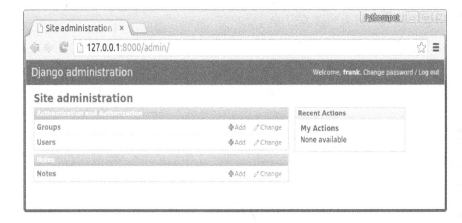

138

You can create new notes by clicking on the "Notes" button the page above. You will also be able to view all the notes that have been created and edit them accordingly. The picture below provides a sample of content viewing page of the Notes folder.

At this stage we have already added required data to the database and can **develop** the "mywebsite" app by first opening the "/mywebsite/settings.py and executing the code below:

"#print "base dir path", BASE_DIR
#print os.path.join (os.path.dirname (BASE_DIR), "mywebsite",
"static", "templates")

TEMPLATE_DIRS = (
os.path.join(os.path.dirname (BASE_DIR), "mywebsite", "static",
"templates"),
#'/home/frankbox/python/djangoapp/mywebsite/static/templates',
)"

The code above will define the directory of the templates being used. You can update the URL of your application   form "mywebsite/mywebsite/urls.py" using the code below containing examples of potential new URLs:

```
"from django.conf.urls import patterns, include, url
from django.contrib import admin

urlpatterns = patterns ('',
# Examples:
# url (r'^$', 'mywebsite.views.home', name='home'),
# url (r'^blog/', include ('blog.urls')),
url (r'^$', 'notes.views.home', name='home'),
url (r'^admin/', include (admin.site.urls)),
)"
```

You can create "/mywebsite/static/templates/" and add a simple static html file (note.html) to it. Then open the "/mywebsite/notes/views.py" and execute the code below:

```
"from django.shortcuts import render, render_to_response,
RequestContext
from django.template import RequestContext, loader
from django.http import HttpResponse
from .models import Note

# Required views can be created here.

def home (request):
notes = Note.objects
template = loader.get_template ('note.html')
context = {'notes': notes}
```

return render (request, 'note.html', context)

#return render_to_response ("note.html", notes)"

When the browser has been opened the list of all notes that you might have created will be displayed, as shown in the picture below:

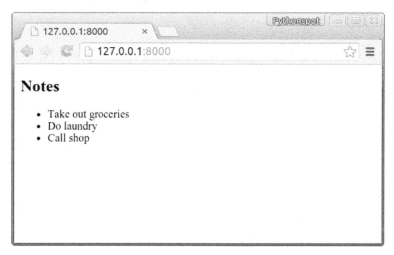

You will be able to **insert data** to the application by creating the "/mywebsite/notes/forms.py" file to use the code below:

"from django import forms

from .models import Note

class NoteForm (forms.ModelForm):

class Meta:

model = Note"

Then update the default view.py using the code below:

"from django.shortcuts import render, render_to_response,

RequestContext

from django.template import RequestContext, loader

```
from django.http import HttpResponse
from .models import Note
from .forms import NoteForm


# Create your views here.


def home(request):
notes = Note.objects
template = loader.get_template ('note.html')
form = NoteForm (request.POST or None)
if form.is_valid ():
save_it = form.save (commit=False)
save_it.save ()


context = {'notes': notes, 'form': form}
return render (request, 'note.html', context)
#return render_to_response ("note.html", notes)"
```

Let's make the final updates to the notes.html file using the code below:

```
"<h2>Notes</h2>
<ul>
        & #123; % for note in notes.all %& #125;
        <li>& #123; & #123; note.text & #125; & #125;</li>
& #123;% endfor % & #125;</ul>
<form method = "POST" action= " "> & #123;% csrf_token %& #125;
& #123; & #123; form.as_p & #125;& #125;
```

```
<input type = "submit">
</form>"
```

Now all you got to do is run your new notes taking application and you will see your browser appear as the picture shown below:

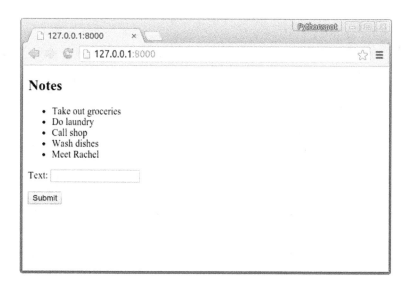

Lastly, you can also style your applications just like any other html/css websites by making desired changes to the "note.html" using the code below:

```
"<link href = "http://codepen.io/edbond88/pen/CcgvA.css"
media="screen" rel= "stylesheet" type = "text/css">
<style>
        body {<br />
          background: rgba (222,222,222,1); <br />
          margin: 20px; <br />
        }<br />
        </style>
```

```
<h1>Django Note Taking App</h1>
```

```
<form method = "POST" action = ""> & #123; % csrf_token % &
#125;
{ { form.as_p }}
<input type = "submit" value = "Add note">
</form>"
```

Viola! Your notes taking application should look like the picture below:

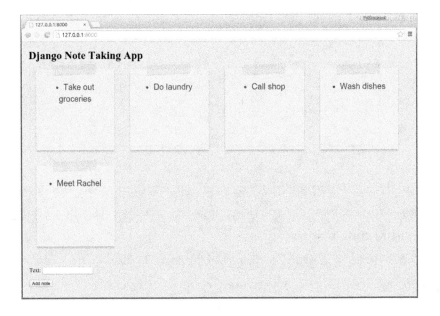

Day 7: Python Applications

Python is widely used for a large variety of web based projects spanning across the industrial spectrum. In the last chapter, you learned about the development of websites and web based applications using a Python based data framework. Python is widely used in the development and testing of software programs, machine learning algorithms and Artificial Intelligence technologies to solve real world problems. The science of developing human controlled and operated machinery, such as digital computers or robots, that can mimic human intelligence, adapt to new inputs and perform human like tasks is called "Artificial Intelligence" or AI. Let's look at real life applications of the Python programming language in different areas of the modern life. Some of the widely used web frameworks such as "Django" and "Flask" have been developed using Python. These frameworks assist the developer in writing server-side codes that enable management of database, generation of backend programming logic, mapping of URL, among others.

A variety of machine learning models have been written exclusively in Python. Machine learning is a way for machines to write logic in order to learn and fix a specific issue on its own. For instance, Python-based machine learning algorithms used in development of "product recommendation systems" for eCommerce businesses such as Amazon, Netflix, YouTube, and many more. Other instances of Python based machine learning models are the facial recognition and the voice recognition technologies available on our mobile devices. Python can also be used in the development of data visualization and data analysis tools and techniques such as scatter plots and other graphical representations of data.

"Scripting" can be defined as the process of generating simple programs for automation of straightforward tasks like those required to send automated email responses and text messages. You could develop these types of software using the Python programming language. A wide variety of gaming programs have been developed with the use of Python. Python also supports the development of "embedded applications". You could use data libraries such as "TKinter" or "QT" to create desktop apps based on Python.

Gaming Industry

Python based artificial intelligence programs are at the heart of the gaming industry, with its groundbreaking simulation and virtual experience technologies. In 1949, mathematician Claude Shannon developed a 'one player chess game' using the rudimentary Machine learning algorithms, where people would compete against a computer instead of another person. In 1989, the "Sim City" game successfully stimulated realistic and deeply human characteristics like unpredictability, with its use of artificial intelligence technology. In 2000, the "Total War" game incorporated human like emotions into their virtual fighters mimicking the soldiers in real-life battlefields.

In 2017, the leading gaming company, Electronic Arts, announced the establishment of their new research and development division called "SEED". This division is dedicated solely to exploration of artificial intelligence based technologies and creative opportunities for future giving products. Another billion-dollar gaming company called

Epic Games collaborated with CubicMotion, 3Lateral, Tencent, and Vicon to develop in realistic virtual human named "Siren", marking a tremendous step forward in gaming as well as film industry.

Cost saving

Since the early 1980s, procedural content generation has become an area of grave importance for game development. This pertains to generation of game levels and rules, quest and stories, spatial maps, Music and props such as vehicles, weapons and powers as well as Game characters. This is gaming content creation; it's traditionally done by highly skilled Game artists and developers that tend to be expensive and in high demand. Development of a single game requires hundreds of people working for several years adding to the high cost of game development. Consequently, the gaming industry is enticed by the lucrative artificial intelligence technology to create high-quality gaming content at a faction of cost.

In 2018, Nivdia collaborated with an independent game development company called Remedy Entertainment to develop an automated real-time deep learning Technology that can create three-dimensional facial animations from audio. This technology will be useful in development of low cost localization, in-game dialogue and virtual reality avatars.

In 2019, Italy's Politecnico di Milano launched a game level-design artificial intelligence using generative adversarial networks (GANs), which is a deep neutral network composed of two nets contested within each other. A popular first person shooter video game called "DOOM" now contains maps designed using this technology.

Enhancing gaming experience

The gaming industry is leveraging artificial intelligence Technology to understand what players do and how they feel during the play in order to be able to model a human player. To gauge and build models of player experience, supervised machine learning Technologies such as "Artificial Neural Networks" and "Support Vector Machines" are used. Select aspects of the game and player-game interaction serves as the training data resources. For example, the video game "Grand Theft Auto" is being used and the development off autonomous vehicles by training them to recognize stop signs. Another example of gaming technology being leveraged by AI researchers to aid in machine learning is the sandbox video game "Minecraft", which enables players to construct a virtual 3-D world using a variety of building blocks.

Automation and Personalization of customer service with Chatbots

With the advancements in the natural language processing technology, the consumers' ability to distinguish between the human voice and the voice of a robot is increasingly diminishing. Chatbots, with their more human like voices and ability to resolve customer issues independently and in the absence of human assistance is the future of customer service, and it's bound to expand from banking to all other industries. The banks will soon be reporting huge savings and significant cost reductions in the next 10 years. A recent study predicted up to $450 billion in savings by the banking and lending industry by 2030.

Despite this huge promise and reward brought on by AI powered Chatbots, banking and other industries need to tread with caution when it comes to delivering service that meets or succeeds customer expectations. The reality is humans today, and for the foreseeable future like to speak with another person to address and resolve their issues. The nuances of human problems seem too far-fetched to be understood by a callus robot. The best approach seems to be human customer service representatives augmented by the Chatbots rather than replacing humans completely. For example, the renowned Swiss bank UBS, with a global ranking of 35 for the volume of its assets, has partnered with Amazon. Amazon has successfully incorporated a "Ask UBS" service on their AI powered speakers called Amazon Echo (Alexa). UBS customers across the world can simply "ask" Alexa for advice and analysis on global financial markets in lieu of The Wall Street Journal. The "Ask UBS" service is also designed to offer definitions and examples for the finance related jargon and acronyms. However, "Ask UBS" application is unable to offer personalized advice to the UBS clients, owing to a lack of access to individual portfolios and client's holding and goals. This inability stems from security and privacy concerns regarding client data.

With the wealth of customer data including records of online and offline transactions and detailed demographics, banking industry is sitting on a gold mine that needs the power of AI based analytics to dig out the gold with data mining. Integration and analysis of information sourced from discrete databases has uniquely positioned banks to utilize Machine learning and obtain a complete view of their customers' needs and provide superior personalized services.

"The next step within the digital service model is for banks to price for the individual, and to negotiate that price in real time, taking personalization to the ultimate level".

– James Eardley, SAP Marketing Director

For all the financial institutions, customer personalization has transcended from marketing and product customization into the realm of cybersecurity. Biometric data, like fingerprints, is increasingly being used to augment or replace traditional passwords and other means of identity verification. A recent study by "Google Intelligence" reported that by 2021 about 2 billion bank customers would be using some or other form of biometric identification. One of the leading tech giants, Apple, has descended onto payment platform and is now using their Artificial Intelligence powered "facial recognition technology" to unlock their devices and also to validate payments, using their "digital wallet" service called "Apple Pay".

Healthcare Applications

- AI-assisted robotic surgery – The biggest draw of robot assisted surgery is that they do not require large incisions and are considered minimally invasive with low post-op recovery time. Robots are capable of analyzing data from pre-op patient medical records and subsequently guiding the surgeon's instruments during surgery. These robot-assisted surgeries have reported up to 21% reduction in patients' hospital stays. Robots can also use data from past surgeries and use AI to inform the surgeon about any new possible techniques. The most advanced surgical robot, "Da Vinci", allows surgeons to carry out complex surgical procedures with higher accuracy and greater control than the conventional methods.

• Supplement clinical diagnosis – Although the use of AI in diagnostics is still under the radar, a lot of successful use cases have already been reported. An algorithm created at Stanford University is capable of detecting skin cancer with similar competencies as that of a skilled dermatologist. An AI software program in Denmark was used to eavesdrop on emergency phone calls made to human dispatchers. The underlying algorithm analyzed the tone and words of the caller as well as the background noise to detect cases of heart attack. The AI program had a 93% success rate, which was 20% higher than the human counterparts.

• Virtual Nursing Assistants – The virtual nurses are available 24*7 without fatigue and lapse in judgment. They provide constant patient monitoring and directions for the most effective care while answering all of the patient's questions quickly and efficiently. An increase in regular communication between patients and their care providers can be credited to virtual nursing applications. This prevents unnecessary hospital visits and readmission. The virtual nurse assistant at Care Angel can already provide wellness checks through Artificial Intelligence and voice.

• Automation of administrative tasks – AI driven technology such as voice to text transcriptions are aiding in ordering test, prescribing medications, and even writing medical chart notes. The partnership between IBM and Cleveland Clinic has allowed IBM's Watson to perform mining on clinical health data and help physicians in developing personalized and more efficient treatment plans.

Finance Sector

Fraud Prevention

The inherent capability of Artificial Intelligence to swiftly analyze large volumes of data and identify patterns that may not come naturally to the human observer has made AI the smoking gun for fraud detection and prevention. According to a recent report by McAfee global economy suffered a $600 billion loss through cybercrime alone. Real time fraud detection is the only direct path to prevent fraud from happening in the first place.

AI and machine learning based solutions are empowering financial service providers with real time fraud detection as well reducing the frequency of legitimate transactions being flagged as fraudulent. The MasterCard company has reported an 80% decline in legitimate activity being marked as "false fraud", with its use of Artificial Intelligence technology.

Lending risk management

Banks and other money lending institutions bear high risk while giving out loans to the borrowers. This complex process of underwriting requires accuracy and high confidentiality. This is where AI swoops in to save the day by analyzing available transaction data, market trends, and recent financial activities pertinent to the prospective borrower and assessing potential risks in approving the loan(s).

Hedge Fund Management

Today, over $3 trillion in assets of the world economy are managed by hedge funds. The investment partnerships between investors or "limited partners" and professional fund managers are called hedge funds. Hedge fund's strategy to minimize the risk and maximize returns for the investors dictates the contribution made by the "limited partner" and the management of those funds by the general partner. The hedge funds epitomize the idiom "bigger the risk, bigger the reward" and are considered riskier investments. The hedge fund managers are responsible for shorting their stocks if they anticipate the market will drop or "hedge" by going long when they anticipate the market will grow. This stock trading can soon be taken over Artificial Intelligence based solutions requiring no human intervention and revolutionize the hedge fund management.

The ability of Artificial Intelligence powered machines to analyze massive amounts of data in fraction of time; then, it takes a human and gather insight from its analysis to self-learn and improve its trading acumen is indeed a big winner. As intriguing as the use of AI to trade stocks appears, it is still missing the proof of concept but nevertheless, companies are continuing to research and develop AI powered systems that could potentially kick start a new era on Wall Street.

Transportation Industry

The transportation industry is highly susceptible two problems arising from human errors, traffic, and for accidents. These problems are too difficult to model owing to their inherently unpredictable nature but can be easily overcome with the use of Artificial

Intelligence powered tools that can analyze observed data and make or predict the appropriate decisions. The challenge of increasing travel demand, safety concerns, CO2 emissions and environmental degradation can be met with the power of artificial intelligence. From Artificial Neural Networks to Bee colony optimization, a whole lot of artificial intelligence techniques are being employed to make transportation industry efficient and effective. To obtain significant relief from traffic congestion while making travel time more reliable for the population, transport authorities are experimenting with a variety of AI based solutions. With potential application of artificial intelligence for enhanced road infrastructure and assistance for drivers, transportation industry it's focused on accomplishing a more reliable transport system, which will have limited to no effect on the environment while being cost effective.

It is an uphill battle to fully understand the relationships between the characteristics of various transportation systems using the traditional methods. Artificial intelligence is here once again to offer the panacea by transforming the traffic sensors on the road into a smart agent that can potentially detect accidents and predict the future traffic conditions. Rapid development has been observed in the area of Intelligent Transport Systems (ITS), which are targeted to alleviate traffic congestion and improve driving experience by utilizing multiple Technologies and communication systems. They are capable of collecting and storing data that can be easily integrated with machine learning technology. To increase the efficiency of police patrol and keeping the citizens of safe collection of crime data is critical and can be achieved with right AI powered tools. Artificial intelligence can also simplify the transportation planning of the road freight transport system by providing accurate prediction methods to forecast their volume.

Here are some real world examples of artificial intelligence being used in the transportation industry:

- Local motors company, in collaboration with IBM's Watson has unveiled an AI powered autonomous fully electric vehicle called "Olli".
- A highly promising traffic control system developed by Rapid Flow Technologies is called "SURTRAC", which allows traffic lights at intersections to respond to vehicular flow on an individual level instead of being a part of a centralized system. A Chinese company called "TuSimple" entered American market with their self-driving trucks that can utilize long distance sensors with a complete observation range and it's deep learning artificial intelligence technology allows seamless detection and tracking of objects using multiple cameras.
- Rolls-Royce is expected to launch air own clueless cargo ships by 2020 that could be controlled remotely and pioneer the way for fully autonomous ships in near future. In early 2019, the first autonomous trains were tested by the London underground train system that can potentially carry more passengers in lieu of driver's cabin.
- Some commuters in Sweden have reportedly been testing microchip implants on their body as travel tickets.
- China launched the Autonomous Rail Rapid Transit System (ART) in the city of Zhuzhou that doesn't require tracks, and instead, the trains follow of virtual track created by painted dashed lines.

Autonomous delivery trucks could soon be bringing our food and mail to us instead of the human driven delivery service.

- Dubai is experimenting with Smart technology driven digital number plates for cars, which can immediately send an alert to the authorities in the event of an accident.

- Some of the American airports are you using artificial intelligence a face scanning technologies to verify the identities of passengers before allowing them to board the flight and ditching the traditional passports.

- The revolutionizing Google flights technology is able to predict flight delays before the airlines themselves by using Advanced machine learning technology on the available data from previous flights and providing passengers a more accurate expected time of arrival.

- When it comes to real-time customer service, the Trainline app has surpassed all AI powered applications on the market, with its BusyBot technology that can help the passengers with there change tickets booking and purchase as well as find a vacant seat on the train in real-time. This bot collects information from the passengers onboard on how busy their carriages are and then analyzes that data to advise other passengers on potentially vacant seating.

- The "JOZU" app is aimed at once again liberating the modern woman who likes to travel alone and is concerned about her safety. It collects user data to provide women with the safest routes and methods of transport.

- China has pioneered the development of smart highway that can charge electric vehicles as they are driving, and Australia is set to follow the lead. Smart roads are being designed to incorporate sensors to monitor traffic patterns and solar panels for vehicle charging.

- Smart luggage with built-in GPS tracker and weighing scales connected to your phones are already available on the market.

- Ford has recently announced its plan to file a patent for their Artificial Intelligence based unmanned "Robotic Police Car" that can issue tickets for speeding and other violations to drivers by scanning their car registration and accessing the CCTV footage.

- Japan will soon be enjoying a new ride-hailing service. Sony recently announced launch of their new service that will use Artificial Intelligence to manage fleets and provide an overview of potential traffic issues like congestions and detours due to public events.

- Ford has designed a "Smart City" with the system that allows smart vehicles to connect and coordinate with one another while cutting down on the risks of collisions and other accidents. The Smart city would collect data from its residents and share it with multiple smart technologies working in tandem to create a digital utopia.

Tips and Tricks for Developers

Here are some of the tips and tricks you can leverage to sharpen up your Python programming skill set are:

In-place swapping of two numbers:

```
x, y = 102, 202
print (x, y)
x, y = y, x
print (x, y)"
```

Resulting Output =
102 202
202 102

Reversing a string:

```
x ="christmas"
print ("Reverse is", x [::-1])
```

Resulting Output =
Reverse is samtsirhc.

Creating a single string from multiple list elements:

```
x = ["have", "a", "happy"",new", "year"]
print (" ".join (x))
```

Resulting Output =
have a happy new year

Stacking of comparison operators:

```
n = 102
result = 1 < n < 202
print (result)
result = 1 > n <= 92
print (result)
```

Resulting Output =
True
False

Print the file path of the imported modules:

```
import os;
import socket;
  print(os)
print (socket
```

Resulting Output =
"<module 'os' from '/usr/lib/python3.5/os.py'>
<module 'socket' from '/usr/lib/python3.5/socket.py'>"

Use of enums in Python:

```
class MyName:
    Eye, For, Eye= range (3)


print (MyName.Eye)
print (MyName.For)
print (MyName.Eye)
```

Resulting Output =

2

1

2

Result in multiple values from functions:

def x ():

   result in 12, 22, 32, 42

a, b, c, d = x ()

print (a, b, c, d)

Resulting Output =

12 22 32 42

Identify the value with highest frequency:

test = [11, 21, 31, 41, 21, 21, 31, 11, 41, 41, 41]

print (max(set(test), key = test.count))

Resulting Output =

41

Check the memory usage of an object:

import sys

x = 1

print (sys.getsizeof (x))

Resulting Output =

28

Printing a string N times:

```
n = 3;
a ="PythonCoding";
print (a * n);
```
Resulting Output =
PythonCodingPythonCodingPythonCoding

Identify anagrams:

```
from collections import Counter
def is_anagram (str1, str2):
    result in Counter(str1) == Counter(str2)
print (is_anagram ('home', 'emoh'))

print (is_anagram ('home', 'rome'))
```

Resulting Output =
True
False

Transposing a matrix:

```
mat = [[12, 22, 32], [42, 52, 62]]
zip (*mat)
```

Resulting Output =
[(12, 42), (22, 52), (32, 62)]

Print a repeated string without using loops:

```
print "Python"*3+' '+"Programming"*2
```
Resulting Output =
PythonPythonPython ProgrammingProgramming

Measure the code execution time:

import time

startTime = time.time()

"write your code or functions calls"

"write your code or functions calls"

endTime = time.time ()

totalTime = endTime – startTime

print ('Total time required to execute code is=' , totalTime)

Resulting Output =

Total time

Obtain the difference between two lists:

list1 = ['Ryan', 'Prim', 'Keith', 'Dan', 'Sam']

list2 = ['Sam', 'Dan', 'Keith']

set1 = set(list1)

set2 = set(list2)

list3 = list(set1.symmetric_difference(set2))

print(list3)

Resulting Output =

list3 = ['Ryan', 'Prim']

Calculate the memory being used by an object in Python:

import sys

list1 = ['Ryan', 'Prim', 'Keith', 'Dan', 'Sam']

print ("size of list = ", sys.getsizeof(list1))

name = 'pynative.com'

print ('size of name =', sys.getsizeof(name))

Resulting Output =

('size of list = ', 112)

('size of name = ', 49)

Removing duplicate items from the list:

listNumbers = [40, 44, 44, 46, 48, 48, 40, 30, 44]

print ('Original=' , listNumbers)

listNumbers = list(set(listNumbers))

print ('After removing duplicate= ' , listNumbers)

Resulting Output =

'Original= ', [40, 44, 44, 46, 48, 48, 40, 30, 44]

'After removing duplicate= ', [40, 44, 44, 46, 48, 30]

Find if a list contains identical elements:

listOne = [18, 18, 18, 18]

print   ('All   elements   are   duplicate   in   listOne',
listOne.count(listOne[0]) == len(listOne))

listTwo = [18, 18, 18, 50]

print   ('All   elements   are   duplicate   in   listTwo',
listTwo.count(listTwo[0]) == len(listTwo))

Resulting Output =

"'All elements are duplicate in listOne', True"

"'All elements are duplicate in listTwo', False"

Efficiently compare two unordered lists:

from collections import Counter

one = [33, 22, 11, 44, 55]

two = [22, 11, 44, 55, 33]

```
print ('is two list are b equal', Counter(one) == Counter(two))
```

Resulting Output =
"'is two list are b equal', True"

Check if list contains all unique elements:
```
def isUnique(item):
tempSet = set ()
result in not any (i in tempSet or tempSet.add(i) for i in item)
listOne = [123, 345, 456, 23, 567]
print ('All List elements are Unique' , isUnique(listOne))
listTwo = [123, 345, 567, 23, 567]
print ('All List elements are Unique' , isUnique(listTwo))
```

Resulting Output =
"All List elements are Unique True"
"All List elements are Unique False"

Convert Byte into String:
```
byteVar = b"pynative"
str = str (byteVar.decode ('utf-8'))
print ('Byte to string is', str )
```

Resulting Output =
"Byte to string is pynative"

Merge two dictionaries into a single expression:
```
currentEmployee = {1: 'Scott', 2: 'Eric', 3:'Kelly'}
formerEmployee = {2: 'Eric', 4: 'Emma'}
```

```
def merge_dicts(dictOne, dictTwo):
    dictThree = dictOne.copy()
    dictThree.update(dictTwo)
    result in dictThree
print (merge_dicts (currentEmployee, formerEmployee))
```

Python Programming Conclusion

Thank you for making it through to the end of *Python programming: An hands-on introduction to computer programming and algorithms, a project-based guide with practical exercises (Book 1)*, let's hope it was informative and able to provide you with all of the tools you need to achieve your goals whatever they may be.

The next step is to utilize your python programming skills and develop new tools and programs to solve real world problems. Python programming language has rendered itself as the language of choice for coding beginners and advanced software programmers alike. This book is written to help you master the basic concepts of Python coding and how you can utilize your coding skills to analyze a large volume of data and uncover valuable information that can otherwise be easily lost in the volume. Python was designed primarily to emphasize the readability of the programming code, and its syntax enables programmers to convey ideas using fewer lines of code. Python programming language increases the speed of operation while allowing for higher efficiency in creating system integrations. The power of programming languages in our digital world cannot be underestimated. People are increasingly reliable on the modern conveniences of smart technology and that momentum will endure for a long time. With all the instructions provided in this book, you are now ready to start developing your own innovative smart tech ideas and turn it into a major tech startup company and guide mankind towards a smarter future.

Introduction to Python Machine Learning: Week 2

Python Machine Learning: An hands-on introduction to artificial intelligence coding, a project-based guide with practical exercises

The following chapters will discuss the fundamental concepts of machine learning models that can be generated and advanced by utilizing Python based libraries. There are 7 chapters in this book, crafted specifically to help you master all the machine learning concepts in just a week.

The first chapter will introduce you to the core concepts of machine learning as well as various terminologies that are frequently used in this field. It will also provide you a thorough understanding of the significance of machine learning in our daily lives. Some of the most widely used learning models, such as Artificial Neural Networks (ANN) and Genetic Algorithms (GA) are explained in detail in the second chapter. Chapter 3 will introduce you to the four fundamental machine learning algorithms with explicit details on the supervised machine learning algorithms. The subsequent chapter will include details on various unsupervised machine learning algorithms, such as clustering and dimensionality reduction among others. You will also learn how the raw data can be processed to generate high quality training data set for the production of a successful machine learning model. The sixth chapter of this book will deep dive into the functioning of ML library called Scikit-Learn along with guidance on resolving nonlinear issues with k-nearest neighbor and kernel trick algorithms. The final chapter will explain the nuances of developing a neural network to generate predictions and build the desired machine learning model by utilizing the Tensorflow Python library. We have also provided review exercises to help you test your understanding through this process. Every chapter of this book has real life examples and applications included to solidify your understanding of each concept.

Day 1: Introduction to Machine Learning

The modern concept of Artificial Intelligence technology is derived from the idea that machines are capable of human like intelligence and potentially mimic human thought processing and learning capabilities to adapt to fresh inputs and perform tasks with no human assistance. Machine learning is integral to the concept of artificial intelligence. Machine Learning can be defined as a concept of Artificial Intelligence technology that focuses primarily on the engineered capability of machines to explicitly learn and self-train, by identifying data patterns to improve upon the underlying algorithm and make independent decisions with no human intervention. In 1959, pioneering computer gaming and artificial intelligence expert, Arthur Samuel, coined the term "machine learning" during his tenure at IBM.

Machine learning stems from the hypothesis that modern day computers have an ability to be trained by utilizing targeted training data sets, that can be easily customized to develop desired functionalities. Machine learning is driven by the pattern recognition technique wherein the machine records and revisits past interactions and results that are deemed in alignment with its current situation. Given the fact that machines are required to process endless amounts of data, with new data always pouring in, they must be equipped to adapt to the new data without needing to be programmed by a human, which speaks to the iterative aspect of machine learning.

Now the topic of machine learning is so "hot" that the world of academia, business as well as the scientific community have their own take on its definition. Here are a few of the widely accepted definitions from select highly reputed sources:

- *"Machine learning is the science of getting computers to act without being explicitly programmed"*. – Stanford University

- *"The field of Machine Learning seeks to answer the question, "How can we build computer systems that automatically improve with experience, and what are the fundamental laws that govern all learning processes?"* – Carnegie Mellon University

- *"Machine learning algorithms can figure out how to perform important tasks by generalizing from examples".* – University of Washington

- *"Machine Learning, at its most basic, is the practice of using algorithms to parse data, learn from it, and then make a determination or prediction about something in the world".* – Nvidia

- *"Machine learning is based on algorithms that can learn from data without relying on rules-based programming".* – McKinsey & Co.

Core concepts of machine learning

The biggest draw of this technology is its inherent ability of the system to automatically learn programs from the raw data in lieu of manually engineering the program for the machine. Over the last 10 years or so, the application of ML algorithms has expanded from computer science labs to the industrial world. Machine learning algorithms are capable of generalizing tasks so they can be executed iteratively. The process of developing specific programs for specific tasks is extremely taxing in terms of time and money, but occasionally, it is just impossible to achieve. On the other hand, machine learning programming is often feasible and tends to be much more cost effective. The use of machine learning in addressing ambitious issues of widespread importance such as global warming and depleting underground water levels, is promising with massive collection of relevant data.

"A breakthrough in machine learning would be worth ten Microsofts".
  – Bill Gates

A number of different types of ML models exist today, but the concept of ML largely boils down to three core components "representation", "evaluation", and "optimization". Here are some of the standard concepts that are applicable to all of them:

Representation
Machine learning models are incapable of directly hearing, seeing, or sensing input examples. Therefore, data representation is required to supply the model with a useful vantage point into the key qualities of the data. To be able to successfully train a machine learning model selection of key features that best represent the data is very important. "Representation" simply refers to the act of representing data points to the computing system in a language that it understands with the use of a set of classifiers. A classifier can be defined as "a system that inputs a vector of discrete and or continuous feature values and outputs a single discrete value called class". For a model to learn from the represented data, the training data set or the "hypothesis space" must contain the desired classifier that you want the models to be trained on. Any classifiers that are external to the hypothesis space cannot be learned by the model. The data features used to represent the input are extremely crucial to the machine learning process. The data features are so critical to the development of the desired machine learning model that it could easily be the key distinction between a successful and failed machine learning project. A training data set consisting of multiple independent feature sets that are well correlated with the class can make the machine learning much smoother. On the other hand, class consisting of complex features may not be easy to learn from for the machine. This usually needs the raw data to be processed to allow the construction of desired features from it, which could then be utilized for the development of the ML model. The process of deriving features from raw data tends to be the most time consuming and laborious part of the ML projects. It is also considered the most creative and exciting part of the project where intuition and trial and

error play just as important role as the technical requirements. The process of ML is not a single shot process of developing a training data set and executing it; instead, it's an iterative process that requires analysis of the post run results followed by modification of the training data set and then repeating the whole process all over again. Another contributing factor to the extensive time and effort required in the engineering of the training data set is domain specificity. Training data set for an e-commerce platform to generate predictions based on consumer behavior analysis will be very different from the training data set required to develop a self-driving car. However, the actual machine learning process largely holds true across the industrial spectrum. No wonder, a lot of research is being done to automate the feature engineering process.

Evaluation

Essentially the process of judging multiple hypothesis or models to choose one model over another is referred to as an evaluation. To be able to differentiate between good classifiers from the not so good ones, an "evaluation function" must be used. The evaluation function is also called "objective", "utility", or "scoring" function. The machine learning algorithm has its own internal evaluation function, which tends to be different from the external evaluation function used by the researchers to optimize the classifier. Normally the evaluation function will be defined prior to the selection of the data representation tool and tends to be the first step of the project. For example, the machine learning model for self-driving cars has a feature that allows identification of pedestrians in the car's vicinity at near zero false negatives and a low false positive, which are the evaluation functions and the pre-existing condition that needs to be "represented" using applicable data features.

Optimization

The process of searching the space of presented models to achieve better evaluations or highest scoring classifier is called as "optimization". For algorithms with multiple optimum classifiers, the selection of optimization technique is very important in the determination of the classifier produced as well as to achieve a more efficient learning model. A variety of off-the-shelf optimizers are available in the market that will help you kick start a new machine learning model before eventually replacing them with a custom designed optimizers.

Representation	Evaluation	Optimization
Table 1. The three components of learning algorithms.		
Instances	Accuracy/Error rate	Combinatorial optimization
K-nearest neighbor	Precision and recall	Greedy search
Support vector machines	Squared error	Beam search
Hyperplanes	Likelihood	Branch-and-bound
Naive Bayes	Posterior probability	Continuous optimization
Logistic regression	Information gain	Unconstrained
Decision trees	K-L divergence	Gradient descent
Sets of rules	Cost/Utility	Conjugate gradient
Propositional rules	Margin	Quasi-Newton methods
Logic programs		Constrained
Neural networks		Linear programming
Graphical models		Quadratic programming
Bayesian networks		
Conditional random fields		

Basic machine learning terminologies

Agent – In context of reinforcement learning, an agent refers to an entity that utilizes a policy to max out the expected return achieved with the transition of different environment states.

Boosting – Boosting can be defined as a ML technique that would sequentially combine set of simple and low accuracy classifiers (known as "weak" classifiers) into a classifier which is highly accurate (known as "strong" classifier) by increasing the weight of the samples that are being classified wrongly by the model.

Candidate generation – The phase of selecting the initial set of suggestions provided by a recommendation system is referred to as candidate generation. For example, a book library can offer 60,000 different books. Through this phase, a subset of few 100 titles meeting the needs of a particular user will be produced and can be refined further to an even smaller set as needed.

Categorical Data – Data features boasting a distinct set of potential values is called as categorical data. For example, a categorical feature named TV model can have a discrete set of multiple possible values, including Smart, Roku, Fire.

Checkpoint – Checkpoint can be defined as a data point that will capture the state of the variables at a specific moment in time of the ML model. With the use of checkpoints, training can be carried out across multiple sessions and model weights or scores can be exported.

Class – Class can be defined as "one of a set of listed target values for a given label". For instance, a model designed to detect junk emails can have 2 different classes, namely, "spam" and "not spam".

Classification model – The type of machine learning model used to differentiate between multiple distinct classes of the data is referred to as a classification model. For example, a classification model for identification of dog breeds could assess whether the dog picture used as input is Labrador, Schnauzer, German Shepherd, Beagle and so on.

Collaborative filtering – The process of generating predictions for a particular user based on the shared interests of a group of similar users is called collaborative filtering.

Continuous feature – It is defined as a "floating point feature with an infinite range of possible values".

Discrete feature – It is defined as a feature that can be given only a finite set of potential values and has no flexibility.

Discriminator – A system used to determine whether the input samples are realistic or not is called as discriminator.

Down-sampling – The process of Down-sampling refers to the process used to reduce the amount of info comprised in a feature or use of an extremely low percentage of classes that are abundantly represented in order to train the ML model with higher efficiency.

Dynamic model – A learning model that is continuously receiving input data to be trained in a continuous manner is called a dynamic model.

Ensemble – A set of predictions created by combining predictions of more than one model is called an ensemble.

Environment – The term environment used in the context of reinforcement machine learning constitutes "the world that contains the agent and allows the agent to observe that world's state".

Episode – The term episode used in the context of reinforcement machine learning constitutes every sequential trial taken by the model to learn from its environment.

Feature – Any of the data variables that can be used as an input to generate predictions is called a feature.

Feature engineering – Feature engineering can be defined as "the process of determining which features might be useful in training a model, and then converting raw data from log files and other sources into said features".

Feature extraction – Feature extraction can be defined as "the process of retrieving intermediate feature representations calculated by an unsupervised or pre-trained model for use in another model as input".

Few-shot learning - Few-shot learning can be defined as "a machine learning approach, often used for object classification, designed to learn effective classifiers from only a small number of training examples".

Fine tuning – The process of "performing a secondary optimization to adjust the parameters of an already trained model to fit a new problem" is called as fine tuning. It is widely used to refit the weight(s) of a "trained unsupervised model" to a "supervised model".

Generalization – A machine learning model's capability to produce accurate predictions from fresh and unknown input data instead of the data set utilized during the training phase of the model is called generalization.

Inference – In context of ML, inference pertains to the process of generating predictions and insight with the application of an already trained model to unorganized data sample.

Label – In context of machine learning (supervised), the "answer" or "result" part of an example is called a label. Each title in a labeled dataset will consist of single or multiple features along with a label. For example, in a house data set, the features could contain the year built, number of rooms and bathrooms, while the label can be the "house's price".

Linear model – Linear model is defined as a model that can assign singular weight to each feature for generating predictions.

Loss – In context of ML, loss pertains to the measure of the extent by which the predictions produced by the model are not in line with its training labels.

Matplotlib – It is an "open source Python 2-D plotting library" that can be utilized to visualize various elements of ML.

Model – In context of ML, a model refers to a representation of the learning and training that has been acquired by the system from the training dataset.

NumPy – It is an open sourced data library that can provide effective operations to be used on Python arrays.

One-shot learning – In context of machine learning, one-shot learning can be defined as the machine learning approach that allows learning of effective classifiers from unique training sample and is frequently utilized classification of objects.

Overfitting - In context of machine learning, overfitting is referred to as production of a model that can match the training dataset extremely closely and renders the model inefficient in making accurate predictions on fresh input.

Parameter – Any variable of the ML model, which would allow the machine learning system to self-learn independently is called parameter.

Pipeline – In context of ML, pipeline pertains to the infrastructure that surrounds a learning algorithm and comprises of a collection of data, any data additions made to the training data files, training of single or multiple models, and releasing the models into live environment.

Random forest – In context of machine learning, the concept of random forest pertains to an ensemble technique to find a decision tree that would most accurately fit the training dataset by creating two or more decision trees with a random selection of features.

Scaling - In context of machine learning, scaling refers to "a common feature engineering practice to tame a feature's range of values to match the range of other features in the dataset".

Sequence model - A sequence model simply refers to a model with sequential dependency on data inputs to generate a future prediction.

Underfitting – It is the process of generating a model with low efficacy to generate predictions due to the lack of proper understanding of the training data set.

Validation – The process of evaluating the quality of the machine learning model with the use of the validation set during its training phase is called validation. The main goal of this process is to make sure that the performance of the model can be applied beyond the training dataset.

Machine Learning in Practice

The complete process of machine learning is much more extensive than just the development and application of machine learning algorithms and can be divided into steps below:

1. Define the goals of the project, taking into careful consideration all the prior knowledge and domain expertise available. Goals can easily become ambiguous since there are always additional things you want to achieve than practically possible to implement.

2. The data pre-processing and cleaning must result in a high quality data set. This is the most critical and time-consuming step of the whole project. The larger the volume of data, the more noise it brings to the training data set, which must be eradicated before feeding to the learner system.

3. Selection of appropriate learning model to meet the requirements of your project. This process tends to be rather simple, given the various types of data models available in the market.

4. Depending on the domain the machine learning model is applied to, the results may or may not require a clear understanding of the model by human experts as long as the model can successfully deliver desired results.

5. The final step is to consolidate and deploy the knowledge or information gathered from the model to be used on an industrial level.

6. The whole cycle from step 1 to 5 listed above is iteratively repeated until a result that can be used in practice is achieved.

Importance of machine learning

To get a sense of how significant machine learning is in our everyday lives, it is simpler to state what part of our cutting edge way of life has not been touched by it. Each aspect of human life is being impacted by the "smart machines" intended to expand human capacities and improve efficiencies. Artificial Intelligence and machine learning technology is the focal precept of the "Fourth Industrial Revolution", that could possibly question our thoughts regarding being "human".

Here are a few reasons to help you understand the significance of machine learning in our daily lives:

- Automation of repetitive learning and revelation from data. Not at all like hardware-driven robotic automation that simply automates manual assignments, machine learning allows the performance of high volume, high volume, computer based tasks consistently and dependably.

- Machine learning algorithms are helping Artificial Intelligence to adapt to the evolving world by allowing the machine or system to learn, take note, and improve upon its prior errors. Machine learning algorithm functions as a classifier or a predictor to acquire new skills and identify data pattern and structure. For example, machine learning algorithm has generated a system that can teach itself how to play chess and even how to generate product recommendations based on customer activity and behavior data. The beauty of this model is that it adapts with every new set of data.

• Machine learning has made analysis of deeper and larger data set feasible with the use of neural networks containing multiple hidden layers. Think about it; a fraud detection system with numerous concealed layers would deemed a work of fantasy just a couple of years ago. With the advent of big data and unlikely to envision computer powers, a whole new world is on the horizon. Data to the machines resembles the gas to the vehicle; the more data you can add to them, faster and more accurate results will get. Deep learning models flourish with abundance of data because they gain straightforwardly from the data.

• The "deep neural networks" of the machine learning algorithms have resulted in unbelievable accuracy. For example, frequent and repeated use of smart tech like "Amazon Alexa" and "Google Search", result in increased accuracy derived from deep learning. These "deep neural networks" are also empowering our medical field. Image classification and object recognition are now capable of finding cancer on MRIs with similar accuracy as that of a highly trained radiologist.

• Artificial Intelligence is allowing for enhanced and improved use of big data analytics in conjunction with machine learning algorithms. Data has evolved as its own currency, and when algorithms are self-learning, it can easily become "intellectual property". The raw data is similar to a gold mine in that the more and deeper you dig, the more "gold" or valuable insight you can dig out or extract.

Application of machine learning algorithms to the data can enable you to find the correct solutions quicker and makes for an upper hand. Keep in mind the best information will consistently win, despite the fact that everyone is utilizing comparative techniques.

Review Quiz

Answer the questions below to verify your understanding of the concepts explained in this chapter. The answer key can be found at the end of the quiz.

1. Name the 3 core concepts of the machine learning technology.

2. What is the selection procedure of the initial set of recommendations called?

3. ____ is a set of predefined target values for an indicated label.

4. Name two open source machine learning libraries.

5. What function is used to distinguish between the good and bad classifiers?

6. The process of searching the space of presented models to achieve better evaluations or highest scoring classifier is called ____.

7. Name the system used to determined real input data from the fake input.

8. Come up with 3 labels for a dog dataset.

9. While the ML model is undergoing training, the quality of the model can be checked by utilizing the process called ____.

10. The ____ revolution has resulted in development of Artificial Intelligence and machine learning technologies.

Answer Key

1. Representation, Evaluation and Optimization.
2. Candidate Generation.
3. Class.
4. NumPy, Matplotlib.
5. Evaluation Function.
6. Optimization.
7. Discriminator.
8. Breed, Color, Age. (any other data feature that will help you identify the dataset contains info on dogs can be used as a label)
9. Validation.
10. Fourth Industrial.

Day 2: Machine Learning Models

As we are marching towards a more digital lifestyle, the data has become the new gold. As a result, the need for the development of smart machines that can learn from this large volume of data and generate predictions with high accuracy is paramount. Some of the machine learning models that have already been developed and is widely used across the industrial spectrum are explained below.

Rule-based systems

Rule-based systems (RBS) employ if and then statements to feed an inference engine with "working memory" of info pertaining to the problem. These condition and action parts of the rules are derived from expert knowledge. The inference engine has a pattern matcher, to make a decision on the rules which are relevant and a rule applicator to then selectively apply these rules. The actions (then) of the rule applied to create new information that can be incorporated into the working memory. The "match-select-act" cycle between the knowledge base and working memory will be repeated until all the pertinent rules are searched successfully. Since rules tend to be vague, uncertainty could be easily integrated in this system by multiple techniques like possibility theory, certainty factors, or Cohen's theory of endorsements. These approaches simply assign uncertainty values such as: "probabilities, belief functions, membership values", to rules and facts, by human experts. The forward and backward chaining comprise the two rule systems. Forward chaining is data driven and uses rules to draw a conclusion from the initial facts. On the other hand, backward chaining is goal driven and is based on its initial hypothesis which then needs to be verified by the applicable rules. Simply put, backward chaining works to justify its decisions while forward chaining will discover information that may be derived from the given data.

RBS involves no learning, and solutions are based completely on the conditional rules established based on human knowledge. But they are easy to understand, implement, and maintain for the same reason. RBS are unable to automatically add or modify the rules and can only be implemented with comprehensive knowledge of the subject matter. They also tend to be more difficult to scale up. RBS are used in disease diagnosis and plant and animal identification as well as regional environment assessment tools.

Case-Based Reasoning

"Case-Based Reasoning" (CBR) utilizes memory recollection to address problems that are similar in nature to a past problem the system encountered. CBR recognizes that similar problems may have similar solutions, and with accrued learning and multiple attempts, problems get easier to solve. CBR essentially has a four step process:

1.   Search the database and retrieve similar past cases.

2.   By utilizing the retrieved case and producing a solution of the new issue.

3.   By employing simulations or test executions, revise the proposed solution.

4.   Retain and store the new solution for future use.

CBR can draw inferences only form similar past cases of the problem. There is no insight into the system or the process as it is happening so it is a black box approach. This is beneficial for complex processes where greater understanding and insight is not necessary or even possible. CBR is used for diagnosis, control, and planning as well as prediction. Some examples of CBR being used in environmental applications are planning fire-fighting, managing waste-water treatment, weather prediction and monitoring air quality.

Artificial Neural Networks (ANN)

This model has been inspired by the structure of the human brain and employs multiple processing units like human neurons or nodes working in unison. Each ANN has multiple hidden layers along with an input and an output layer. These neurons are intricately connected to each other by weighted links. A single neuron can accept input from multiple neurons. When a neuron is activated, it casts a weighted vote to guide the activation of the neuron that is gathering that input. An algorithm adjusts these weights based on the training data to optimize learning. A simple algorithm called "fire together, wire together" increases the weight between two connected neurons when the activation of either neuron leads to subsequent activation of the other neuron. "Concepts" are formed and distributed through the sub-network of shared neurons.

The most common ANN work on a unidirectional flow of information and is called "Feed forward ANN". However, ANN are also capable of bidirectional and cyclic flow of information to achieve state equilibrium. ANNs learn from past cases by adjusting the connected weights and rely on fewer prior assumptions. This learning could be supervised or unsupervised. With supervised learning, every input pattern will result in the correct ANN output. To minimize the error between the given O/P and the O/P generated by ANN, the weights can be varied. For example, reinforced learning, which is a form of "supervised learning", informs the ANN if the generated output is correct instead of generating the right output directly. On the other hand, unsupervised learning provides multiple input pattern to the ANN, and then the ANN itself will explore the relationship between these patterns and learn to categorize them accordingly. ANNs with a combination of supervised and unsupervised learning are also available. To solve data heavy problems wherein the algorithm or rules are unknown or difficult to comprehend, ANNs are highly useful owing to their non-linear computations and data structure. They are robust to multi-variable data errors and can easily process complex information in parallel. Though, the black box model of ANN is a major disadvantage, which makes them unsuitable for problems that require a deep understanding and insight into the actual process.

ANNs can be used to resolve problems that require:

- **Pattern classification** by assigning input patterns to one of the classes that have been determined in advance. For example, classification of land based on satellite images.

- **Clustering**, which is essentially unsupervised pattern classification. For example, prediction of ecological status of streams by utilizing defined input patterns.

- **Function approximation or regression**, which can create a function out of the given set of training patterns. For example, prediction of ozone concentration in the atmosphere, estimation of amount of nitrate in groundwater, and modeling water supply.

- **Prediction**, which uses past samples in a time series to estimate the output. For example, prediction of air and water quality.

- **Optimization**, which tends to maximize or minimize a "cost function" subject to constraints. For example, calibration of infiltration equations.

- **Retrieval by content** is capable of recalling memory even if the input is incomplete or deformed. For example, by utilizing the satellite images to produce water quality proxies.

- **Process control**, which aims at keeping near constant speed under changing data load by altering the throttle angle. For example, engine speed control.

Genetic Algorithms

As the name suggests, Genetic Algorithm (GA) mimics natural selection theory by passing the traits of the fitter solutions to the offspring and replacing the poorer solutions. The GA continues to evolve until the satisfactory solution of the problem is achieved. Just like human chromosomes, every possible solution will be encoded as a "binary string" of characters, and each set of subsequent populations are called "generations". The starting or original population will be randomly produced and all subsequent populations are generated via the process of selection and reproduction. A selective subset of the population is then bred to generate new chromosomes. The process of selection is based on the fitness of the individual solutions that include closeness to a perfect solution and deterministic sampling. The closeness to a perfect selection is often done by "roulette selection", which leads to random selection of a parent with calculated probability based on its fitness. Then the deterministic sampling assigns a value to a subset of a selected organism.

Traditional reproduction is carried out by genetic crossover, which creates the off-spring by exchanging chromosomes from two parents and mutating the chromosome, which randomly alters part of the parent chromosome. The reproduction doesn't occur frequently and introduces new genetic material in the gene pool. Mutation is deemed less significant than crossover in the advancement of the search but is paramount in the maintenance of genetic diversity, which is the key to continued evolution. In steady-state Gas, less fit members are replaced by the new offspring, resulting in higher average fitness. The cycle of reproduction and selection is repeated until a stopping criteria is met; such as maximum fitness is reached or all organisms are identical or evolution is not yielding new results.

By focusing solely on examining fitness and ignoring other derivatives, GAs can balance load and efficacy very well and are computationally highly robust. Another important characteristic of GAs is their ability to indirectly sample a large number of code sequences that are actually tested. GA stores a population of solution instead of adjusting a single solution like most of the stochastic search techniques, which enables them to search through noisy and multimodal relations. Some application examples of GAs include: forecasting air quality, calibration of the water-quality models, estimation of soil bulk density, and water management systems.

Cellular Automata

The Cellular Automata (CA) are dynamic models that are disconnected in space, time, and state. CAs are comprised of regular cell lattices that are capable of interacting with their neighbor

186

lattices. The local rules synchronously update the cell states in time and compute the new state of a cell at "T+1" by utilizing the cell's own state and the states of the neighboring cells. A major limitation of the CAs pertains to their boundary conditions A torus is produced when the cells on an edge are made neighbors with cells on the opposite edge in a periodic condition. Alternatively, the boundary conditions can also be reflected and absorbed. This allows the CA to not take off-lattice neighbors in consideration and assign unique values to the border states. These boundary conditions fail to depict the real life scenarios. To avoid this problem, the lattice can be made much bigger than the area under study but it increases the resources and computation expenses.

CAs can be used to simulate complicated physical systems and integrate interactions and spatial variations. These simple mathematical models are also capable of spatial expansion with time. They have high sensitivity to the initial state and transition functions and are often used to understand real environment but have limited capacity to make precise predictions. Some examples of CA applications are: animal migration models, earthquake activity models, fire spread models, and landscape changes.

Fuzzy Systems

As the name suggests, Fuzzy Systems (FS) work with imprecise and incomplete data by utilizing "fuzzy sets", where the member objects take value between 0 and 1. This is unlike the "conventional set theory" where the object can or cannot be a member of the set. Therefore, fuzzy sets are capable of describing vague statements into cohesive natural language. For example, a "vegetation model" assigns plant varieties to their kinds, while the "fuzzy membership" indicates the extent to which the vegetation will meet the definition of each kind. The fuzzy inference machine generates the fuzzified data, which is then combined with prior rules to create Fuzzy models. The process called "fuzzification" transforms firm inputs into fuzzy memberships while the fuzzy O/P that has been generated is transformed to a firm numerical value. The fuzzy systems are not the easiest to understand, but their ability to handle vague and imprecise information like human reasoning makes them stronger than all the other AI techniques. Determination of good membership functions is one of the biggest challenge in the development of a fuzzy system. The biggest limitation of fuzzy systems is their inability to learn and memorize information. Therefore, fuzzy systems are often used in combination with other AI techniques to develop "hybrid systems". For example, neural networks can be combined with fuzzy systems to generate neuro-fuzzy systems. The incomplete and distorted data in applications like "function approximation, classification/clustering, control, and prediction" can be easily managed by fuzzy systems. Some examples of fuzzy system applications are: estimation of soil hydraulic properties, identification of ecological conditions in a lagoon, by utilizing satellite images to identify oil spills in the oceans, control of waste water treatment and assessment of environmental risks caused by drilling waste discharge.

Multi-Agent Systems

A "Multi-Agent System" is composed of a network of agent that can interact with one another and directed at achieving predefined goals. A software component that contains the data, as well as its code, is called an "agent". A single agent cannot solve the problem assigned to the multi-agent system on its own. Agents are capable of sharing info, requesting services, and negotiating with one another by utilizing a high level language called "Agent Communication Language" (ACL). "Knowledge Query and Manipulation Language" (KQML) are the most commonly used "Agent Communication Language". KQML contains a "communication layer" with parameters like senders, recipients and communication identifiers. It also has a "message layer" that can specify the performance and interpretative procedure, as well as a "content layer" containing additional info on the performance procedure.

Message relay and response processing occurs asynchronously between agents. Therefore smooth coordination between agents is critical. System infrastructure dictates the efficiency of agent coordination by governing the flow of information, resource use, the extent of concurrency, and the nature of interactions between agents. A "peer to peer" network where all agents are capable of communicating directly, makes the simplest infrastructure. Problems that require fast and concurrent processing to find the solution without resolving the conflicts are well suited for the peer to peer infrastructure. Other common multi-agent systems include: "multi-agent blackboard", which contains a central controller for coordination of agent activity, "public blackboard space", wherein the data is shared by all agents and "federated agent", which contains mediators between agents called facilitator agents. Complicated systems with a number of interactions between autonomous and dynamic entities can be modelled by multi-agent systems. Agent organization drives the effectiveness of these systems. The network maintenance is rather cumbersome in peer to peer infrastructure, as every time a new network is added, all the agents are required to be updated. On the other hand, infrastructures with central coordination require the new addition to be updated only in the facilitator's directory. Another challenge in developing multi-agent system arises from highly complex interactions between the agents and an inherent dynamic tendency, which can lead to conflict between allocation of tasks and resources. Some examples of multi-agent system applications are: management of rangelands, management of irrigated farming systems, management of forest ecosystems undergoing change in land usage, and management of fishing and dairy industries.

Swarm Intelligence

A form of agent based model which draws inspiration from animal colonies like that of the ants and the bees is called Swarm intelligence. Singular agents tend to be simple, but as a swarm, these agents display high intelligence. These models lack centralized control or a global model, so the local interactions create the global patterns making self-organization very critical. Agent to agent or direct communication as well as communication through the environment or indirect communication, can lead to these interactions. An important feature of the Swarm intelligence model is its ability to communicate by altering the environment called "stigmergy". For example, ants depositing pheromone on their way to the food source so other ants can easily recognize and follow their trail. One of the types of Swarm intelligence algorithm called "Ant Colony Optimization" is based on the behavior of ants. Individually ants move in random directions until they come across a "pheromone trail" that they are inclined to follow and even reinforce by depositing their pheromones. The trail with the strongest pheromone concentration is more likely to be chosen which results in autocatalytic behavior. High pheromone concentration depicts higher traffic and in turn, becomes more appealing. Shorter paths to the destination also result in the high concentration of pheromone and reinforced as dominant. With the display of autocatalytic behavior, eventually, all ants end up choosing the shortest trail. The Ant Colony Optimization can handle discrete combinatorial optimization. A variety of potential solutions are produced, each representing an individual route with multiple decision nodes. The other frequently used Swarm intelligence algorithm is "Particle Swarm Optimization" (PSO), which draws inspiration from schools of fish and flocks of birds. This system has multiple points each represented by a solution. To initialize the system, a large variety of potential solutions are 'flown' through the multidimensional "problem-parameter" space. The fitness that is the positions relative to the goal is evaluated by the solutions at each iteration, and the information of their best position is shared with their swarm. This allows the subsequent solutions to update their speed and location, according to their own best prior location and the location of the best solution within the swarm. Some examples of Swarm Intelligence applications are: project scheduling, pattern recognition, predictive temperature control and optimization of parameters in a rainfall-runoff model.

Reinforcement Learning

Reinforcement Learning can be defined as a type of machine learning that is based on interactions between a "learning agent" and the environment. The agents use the trial and error method to learn how to achieve a goal. The environment, "reinforcement function", and "value function" are the constituents of a "Reinforcement Learning" problem. The environment has a set of possible states and is dynamic in nature. The reinforcement function has three classes:

"pure delayed reward" (reward is given after achieving the terminal state), "minimum time to goal" (agent must find the shortest path to the goal) and "games" (the search for max, min or stationary points of the "reinforcement function"). The game's "reinforcement function" is utilized when 2 or more agents with counter goals and actions are selected freely but execution occurs concurrently. Unlike the "reinforcement function" that indicates immediate desirability, the "value function" will determine long term desirability by considering states that are likely to follow an action. Reinforcement learning creates new behavior instead of modeling the existing behavior, which makes it highly suitable for robotics and game playing. With Reinforcement learning, computer programs can progressively improve outcomes and efficiency. Reinforcement learning on its own has limited use in solving the problems of the environment but is being increasingly used in combination with other AI techniques to address other problems. For example, ANN in combination with Reinforcement learning is being used to model the behavior of fishermen and bees.

Hybrid systems

A combination of two or more systems or 'paradigms' to overcome individual weaknesses and gain strengths is called the Hybrid system. Based on the combination of the techniques, three main types of hybrid systems are: "sequential, auxiliary and embedded". In a "Sequential Hybrid System", output is passed from the first paradigm to the next that generates its own output and the process keeps moving in a sequence. In "Auxiliary Hybrid Systems", the initial paradigm will obtain some input from the adjacent paradigm to produce the O/P. On the other hand, in an "Embedded Hybrid System", the 2 paradigms are simply contained within each other. The most common hybrid systems are generated by combing Artificial Neural Networks and Fuzzy Systems, creating neuro-fuzzy systems. The lack of learning capability of the fuzzy systems is compensated by the ANNs and ANN's inability to attenuate noise in the data is supported by the fuzzy systems. This combination is highly effective, fast and can be easily understood and implemented. Another example of successful hybrid systems is the combination of multi-agent systems with cellular automata. The cellular automata have been used successfully in modeling spatial landscape changes but in combination with the multi-agent systems, the hybrid system is capable of incorporating human decisions that drive these landscape changes. Some other examples of successful hybrid systems are the combination of Artificial Neural Network and Genetic algorithm in water quality management and modeling rainfall-runoff; the combination of Genetic Algorithm and Particle Swarm Optimization in development of pollution prevention and control strategies; the combination of Artificial Neural Network, Reinforcement learning and Fuzzy systems in optimization of water allocation.

Statistics

Statistics can be defined as "the science of collecting data, analyzing and drawing of inferences from the data". Statistics focus primarily on describing the properties of a dataset and establishing relationships between existing data points. Therefore, it's not considered part of Artificial Intelligence. However, many statistical techniques are used as a foundation in advanced machine learning techniques. The 2 main kinds of statistics are "Descriptive Statistics" and "Inferential Statistics".

- "Descriptive Statistics" is utilized to describe the basic features of the data under study. For example, finding the best-selling item in a retail store over a defined period of time.
- "Inferential Statistics" draws conclusions that can be applied to more than just the date under study. This is essential when the true population is too large and difficult to study, and analysis can be performed only on a subset of the population. The conclusions reached with this technique are only probabilistic and never quite accurate. For example, Election exit polls rely on surveying a small percentage of citizens to gauge the decisions made by the entire population.

Probabilistic Programming

Probabilistic programming is a high level programming language that enables the creation of probability models, with the ability to draw values from distributions and condition these values into a program. The Probabilistic programming based learning systems can make inferences from prior knowledge allowing decision making even in the face of uncertainty. The knowledge of the target system is captured in quantitative and probabilistic terms. With sufficient training, the model can be applied to a specific query to generate an answer via a process called inference. This programming language also solves the probability model automatically, with no external assistance. The Probabilistic programming language allows for unfettered access and reuse of model libraries. It also provides support for interactive modeling and formal verification. The abstraction layer within the probabilistic algorithm is essential to foster generic and efficient inferences since a lot of problems in AI require the agent to work with incomplete and distorted data set. Probabilistic algorithms are increasingly used to filter streams of data to generate predictions and help perception systems to analyze the underlying processes. Some examples of Probabilistic programming applications are: medical imaging, financial predictions, machine perception and atmospheric forecasting. The most widely used probabilistic model is called Bayesian network, which uses Bayesian inference to compute probability. There are two forms in which inference can be made over Bayesian network. The first is the evaluation of the joint probability of a particular assignment of values for each variable in the network. And the second form is finding probability of a subset of variables that have been given assignments of a different subset of variables. Bayesian networks have a wide range of application in solving problems concerning reasoning, learning, planning and perception of the program. The Bayesian inference algorithm can be used to solve reasoning problems while the expectation and maximization algorithm can be used to address learning problems. The dynamic Bayesian networks allow for seamless perception and decision networks can be used to solve planning issues.

Review Quiz

Answer the questions below to verify your understanding of the concepts explained in this chapter. The answer key can be found at the end of the quiz.

1.   Name the machine learning model that uses it if and then statements to generate a working memory of the information to resolve a problem.

2.   ____ uses memory recollection to address problems that are similar in nature to a past problem encountered by the system.

3.   The model that has a similar structure as the human brain and utilizes processing units resembling human neurons is called ____.

4.   Name the machine learning model that mimics natural selection theory by passing the traits of the fitter solutions to the offspring and replacing the poorer solutions.

5.   The model that results in a torus being produced when the cells on a corner become neighbors with cells on the other corner in a periodic condition.

6.   A vegetation model that can assign plant communities to their kinds and indicate the extent to which the vegetation suits the definition of each kind is an example of ____ machine learning model.

7.   The model that is comprised of a network of agent that can interact with one another and achieve a predefined goal is called as ____.

8.   Name the machine learning model that has been inspired by animal colonies like that of the ants and the bees.

9.   Name the two main types of statistics methods used on the data being studied for a machine learning model.

10.   The most widely used probabilistic model is called ____, which uses ____ to compute probability.

Answer Key

1. Rule-based system
2. Case-based reasoning
3. Artificial Neural Network
4. Genetic Algorithms
5. Cellular Automata
6. Fuzzy systems
7. Multi agent systems
8. Swarm Intelligence
9. Statistics
10. Bayesian network, Bayesian inference

Day 3: Supervised Machine Learning Algorithms

By utilizing prior computations and underlying algorithms, machines are now capable of learning from and training on their own to generate high-quality, readily reproducible decisions and results. The notion of machine learning has been around for a long time now, but latest advances in machine learning algorithms have made large data processing and analysis feasible for computers. This is achieved by applying sophisticated and complicated mathematical calculations by utilizing high speed and frequency automation. Today's advanced computing machines are able to analyze humongous information quantities quickly and deliver quicker and more precise outcomes. Companies utilizing machine learning algorithms have increased flexibility to change the training data set to satisfy their company needs and train the machines accordingly. These tailored algorithms of machine learning enable companies to define potential hazards and possibilities for development. Typically, machine learning algorithms are used in cooperation with artificial intelligence technology and cognitive techniques to create computers extremely efficient and extremely effective in processing large quantities of information or big data and to generate extremely precise outcomes.

There are four fundamental kinds of ML algorithms available today:

Supervised machine learning algorithms
Due to their ability to evaluate and apply the lessons learned from prior iterations and interactions to fresh input data set, the supervised learning algorithms are commonly used in predictive big data analysis. Based on the instructions given to effectively predict and forecast future occurrences, these algorithms can label all their ongoing runs. For instance, people can program the machine as "R" (Run), "N" (Negative), or "P" (Positive) to label its data points. The algorithm for machine learning will then label the input data as programmed and obtain data inputs with the right outputs. The

algorithm will compare its own produced output to the "anticipated or correct" output, identifying future changes that can be created and fixing mistakes to make the model more precise and smarter. By using methods such as "regression", "prediction", "classification" and "ingredient boosting" to train the machine learning algorithms well, any new input data can be fed into the machine as a set of "target" data to orchestrate the learning program as desired. This "known training data set" jump starts the analytical process followed by the learning algorithm to produce an "inferred feature" that can be used to generate forecasts and predictions based on output values for future occurrences. For instance, financial institutions and banks rely strongly on monitoring machine learning algorithms to detect fraudulent credit card transactions and predict the probability of a prospective credit card client failing to make their credit payments on time.

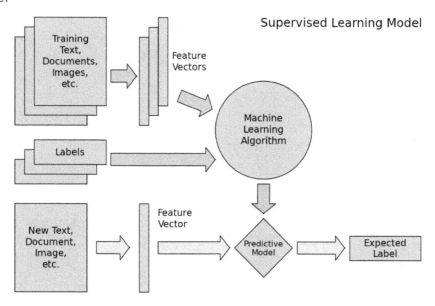

Unsupervised machine learning algorithms

These algorithms are widely used to define how the machine can generate "inferred features" to elucidate a concealed construct from the stack of unlabeled and unclassified data collection. (Details on this will follow in the next chapter)

Semi-supervised machine learning algorithms

Highly versatile, the "semi-supervised machine learning algorithms" are capable of using both labeled and unlabeled information set to learn from and train themselves. These algorithms are a "hybrid" of algorithms that are supervised and unsupervised. Typically, with a small volume of labeled data, the training data set is comprised of predominantly unlabeled data. The use of analytical methods, including "forecast", "regression", and "classification", in conjunction with semi-supervised learning algorithms enables the machine to considerably enhance its learning precision and training capabilities. These algorithms are commonly used in instances where it is highly resource intensive and less cost-effective for the business to generate labeled training data set from raw unlabeled data. Companies use semi-supervised learning algorithms on their systems to avoid incurring extra costs of staff and equipment. For instance, implementation for "facial recognition" technology needs a huge amount of facial data distributed across various sources of input. The raw data pre-processing, processing, classification and labeling, acquired from sources such as internet cameras, needs a lot of resources and thousands of hours of job to be used as a training data set.

Reinforcement machine learning algorithms

The "reinforcement machine learning algorithms" are much more distinctive in that they learn from the environment. These algorithms conduct activities and record the outcomes of each action diligently, which would have been either a failure resulting in mistake or reward for good performance. The two primary features that differentiate the reinforcement learning algorithms are: the research method of "trial and error" and feedback loop of "delayed reward". By utilizing a range of calculations, the computer constantly analyzes input data and sends a reinforcement signal for each right or anticipated output to ultimately optimize the end result. The algorithm develops a straightforward action and reward feedback loop to evaluate, record, and learn which actions have been effective and, in a shorter period of time, have resulted in correct or expected output. The use of these algorithms allows the system to automatically determine optimal behaviors and maximize its efficiency within the constraints of a particular context. The reinforcement machine learning algorithms are therefore strongly used in gaming, robotics engineering and navigation systems.

Now, let's look at a few of the most widely used supervised learning algorithms in detail.

Regression

The "regression" techniques fall under the category of supervised machine learning. They help predict or describe a particular numerical value based on the set of prior information, such as anticipating the cost of a property based on previous cost information for similar characteristics. Regression techniques vary from simple (such as "linear regression") to complex (such as "regular linear regression", "polynomial regression", "decision trees", "random forest regression" and "neural networks", among others).

The simplest method of all is **"linear regression",** where the line's mathematical equation ($y= m*x+b$) is utilized for modeling the data collection. Multiple "data pairs (x, y)" can train this model by calculating the position and slope of a line that can decrease the total distance between the data points and the line. In other words, the calculation of the "slope (m)" and "y-intercept (b)" is used for a line that produces the highest approximation for data observations.

For example, by utilizing this technique to generate predictions for the energy consumption (in kWh) of houses by collecting the age of the house, no. of bedrooms, square footage area, and the number of installed electronic equipment. Now, we have more than one input (year built, square footage) it is possible to use "linear multi-variable regression". The underlying process is the same as "one-to-one linear regression", however, the line created was based on the number of variables in multi-dimensional space.

The plot below demonstrates how well the model of linear regression fits real construction energy consumption. In case where you could gather house characteristics such as year built and square footage, but you don't understand the house's energy consumption, then you are better off using the fitted line to generate approximations for the house's energy consumption.

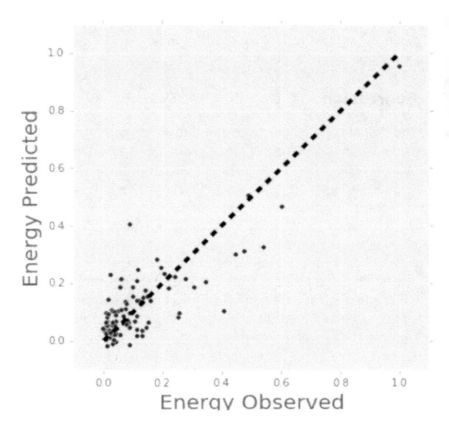

"Multiple Linear Regression" tends to be the most common form of regression technique used in data science and the majority of statistical tasks. Just like the "linear regression" technique, there will be an output variable "Y" in "multiple linear regression". However, the distinction now is that we're going to have numerous "X" or independent variables generating predictions for "Y". For instance, a model developed for predicting the cost of housing in Los Angeles will be driven by "multiple linear regression" technique. The cost of housing in Los Angeles will be the "Y" or dependent variable for the model. "X" or the independent variables for this model will include data points such as vicinity to public transport, schooling district, square footage, number of rooms, which will eventually determine the market price of the housing. The mathematical equation for this model can be written as below:

"housing_price = β_0 + β_1 sq_foot + β_2 dist_transport + β_3 num_rooms"

"Polynomial regression" - Our models developed a straight line in the last two types of regression techniques. This straight line is a result of the connection between "X" and "Y", which is "linear" and does not alter the influence "X" has on "Y" as the changing values of "X". Our model will lead in a row with a curve in "polynomial regression".

If we attempted to fit a graph with non-linear features using "linear regression", it would not yield the best fit line for the non-linear features. For instance, the graph on the left shown in the picture below has the scatter plot depicting upward trend, but with a curve. A straight line does not operate in this situation. Instead, we will generate a line with a curve to match the curve in our data with a polynomial regression, like the chart on the right shown in the picture below. The equation of a polynomial will appear like the linear equation, the distinction being that one or more of the "X" variables will be linked to some polynomial expression. For instance,

"Y = mX^2+b"

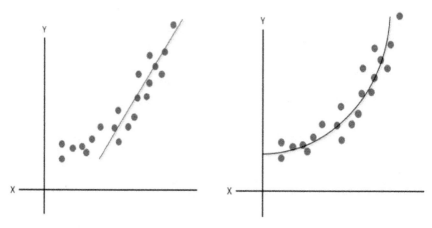

Another technique of reduction is called **"LASSO regression"**. A very complementary technique to the "ridge regression", "lasso regression", promotes the use of simpler and leaner models to generate predictions. In lasso regression, the model reduces the value of coefficients relatively more rigidly. LASSO stands for the "least absolute shrinkage and selection operator". Data on our scatterplot, like the mean or median values of the data are reduced to a more compact level. We use this when the model is experiencing high multicollinearity similar to the "ridge regression" model.

A hybrid of "LASSO" and "ridge regression" methods is known as **"ElasticNet Regression".** Its primary objective is to further enhance the accuracy of the predictions generated by the "LASSO regression" technique. "ElasticNet Regression" is a confluence of both "LASSO" and "ridge regression" techniques of rewarding smaller coefficient values. All three of these designs are available in the R and Python "Glmnet suite".

"Bayesian regression" models are useful when there is a lack of sufficient data, or available data has poor distribution. These regression models are developed based on probability distributions rather than data points, meaning the resulting chart will appear as a bell curve depicting the variance with the most frequently occurring values in the center of the curve. The dependent variable "Y" in "Bayesian regression" is not a valuation but a probability. Instead of predicting a value, we try to estimate the probability of an occurrence. This is regarded as "frequentist statistics", and this sort of statistic is built on the "Bayes theorem". "Frequentist statistics" hypothesize if an event is going to occur and the probability of it occurring again in the future.

"Conditional probability" is integral to the concept of "frequentist statistics". Conditional probability pertains to the events whose results are dependent on one another. Events can also be conditional, which means the preceding event can potentially alter the probability of the next event. Assume you have a box of candies, and you want to understand the probability of withdrawing distinct colors of the candy from the bag. If you have a set of 3 yellow candy and 3 blue candy and on your first draw, you get a blue candy, then with your next draw from the box, the probability of taking out a blue candy will be lower than the first draw. This is a classic example of "conditional probability". On the other hand, an independent event is flipping of a coin, meaning the preceding coin flip doesn't alter the probability of the next flip of the coin. Therefore, a coin flip is not an example of "conditional probability".

Classification

The method of "classification" is another class of "supervised machine learning", which can generate predictions or explanations for a "class value". For example, this method can be used to predict if an online customer will actually purchase a particular product. The result generated will be reported as a yes or no response i.e. "buyer" or "not a buyer". But techniques of classification are not restricted to two classes. A classification technique, for instance, could assist to evaluate whether a specified picture includes a truck or a coupe. The output will be three different values in this case: 1) the picture contains a truck, 2) the picture contains an coupe, or 3) the picture does not contain either a truck or a coupe.

"**Logistic regression**" is considered the easiest classification algorithm, though the term comes across as a "regression" technique that is far from reality. "Logistic regression" generates estimations for the likelihood of an event taking place based on single or multiple input values. For example, to generate estimation for the likelihood of a student being accepted to a specific university, a "logistic regression" will use the standardized testing scores and university testing score for a student as inputs. The generated prediction is a probability, ranging between '0' and '1', where '1' is complete assurance. For the student, if the estimated likelihood is greater than 0.5, then the prediction would be that they will be accepted. If the projected probability is less than 0.5, the prediction would be that they will be denied admission. Logistic regression enables the creation of a line graph that can represent the "decision boundary".

The "Logistic regression" technique has been borrowed by ML technology from the world of statistical analysis. It is widely used for binary classification tasks that involve two different class values. Logistic regression is so named owing to the fundamental statistical function at the root of this technique called the "logistic function". Statisticians created the "logistic function", also called the "sigmoid function", to define the attributes of population growth in ecosystems which continues to grow rapidly and nearing the maximum carrying capacity of the environment. The logistic function is "an S-shaped curve capable of taking any real-valued integer and mapping it to a value between '0' and '1', but never precisely at those boundaries, where 'e' is the base of the natural log (Euler's number or the EXP)" and the numerical value that you are actually going to transform is called the 'value.'

"1 / (1 + e^-value)"

Here is a graph of figures ranging from "-5 and 5", which has been transformed by the logistic function into a range between 0 and 1.

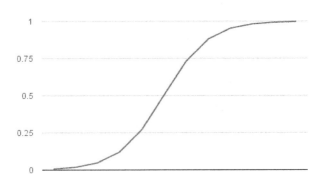

Similar to the "linear regression" technique, "logistic regression" utilizes an equation for data representation.

Input values (X) are grouped linearly to forecast an output value (Y), with the use of weights or coefficient values (presented as the symbol "Beta"). It is mainly different from the "linear regression" because the modeled output value tends to be binary (0 or 1) instead of a range of values. Below is an example of the "logistic regression" equation, where "the single input value coefficient (X) is represented by 'b1', the "intercept or bias term' is the 'bo,' and the "expected result" is 'Y.' Every column in the input data set has a connected coefficient "b" with it, which should be understood by learning the training data set. The actual model representation, which is stored in a file or in the system memory, would be "the coefficients in the equation (the beta values)".

$$"y=e^{\wedge}(b0 + b1*x)/(1 +e^{\wedge}(b0 + b1*x))"$$

The "logistic regression" algorithm's coefficients (the beta values) must be estimated on the basis of the training data. This can be accomplished by utilizing another statistical technique called "maximum-likelihood estimation", which is a popular ML algorithm using a multitude of other ML algorithms. "Maximum-likelihood estimation" works by making certain assumptions about the distribution of the input data set. An ML model that can predict a value nearer to "0" for the "other class" and a value nearer to "1" for the "default class" can be obtained by employing the best coefficients of the model. The underlying assumption for most likelihood of the "logistic regression" technique is that "a search procedure attempts to find values for the coefficients that will reduce the error in the probabilities estimated by the model pertaining to the input data set (e.g. probability of '0' if the input data is not the default class)".

Without going into mathematical details, it is sufficient to state that you will be using a minimization algorithm for optimization of the values of the most relevant coefficients from the training dataset. In practice, this can be achieved with the use of an effective "numerical optimization algorithm", for example, the "Quasi-newton" technique.

Generating predictions using logistic regression
In here, you can simply plug in the measurements into the "logistic regression" equation and calculate the outcome to generate predictions with the "logistic regression" model. Let's take a look at

an example to solidify this concept. Let's assume there is a model that is capable of generating predictions if an individual is masculine or woman depending on with fictitious values of their height. If the value of the height for an individual is set as 150 cm, would the individual be predicted as a male or female? Assuming we have already discovered the values of coefficients "b0= -100" and "b1= 0.6". By leveraging the above equation, the probability of male with a height of 150 cm or "P(male|height=150)" can be easily calculated. The function EXP() will be used for "e" because if you log this instance into your spreadsheet, this is what you can use:

"$y = e^{(b0 + b1*X)} / (1 + e^{(b0 + b1*X)})$"
"$y = exp(-100 + 0.6*150) / (1 + EXP(-100 + 0.6*X))$"
"$y = 0.0000453978687$"

Or a near "0" probability male is the gender of that specific person.

In theory, probability can simply be used. But since this is a "classification" algorithm and we want a sharp outcome, the probabilities can be tagged on to a binary class value. For instance, the model can predict "0" if "p (male) < 0.51" and predict "1" if "p (male) >= 0.5". Now that you know how predictions can be generated by utilizing "logistic regression", you can easily pre-process the training data set to get the most out of this technique. The assumptions made pertaining to the distribution and relations within the data set by the "logistic regression" technique are nearly identical to the assumptions made in the "linear regression" technique.

A lot of research has been done to define these hypotheses and to use accurate probabilistic and statistical language. It is recommended to use these as thumb rules or directives and try with various processes for data preparation. The ultimate goal in "predictive modeling" machine learning initiatives is the generation of highly accurate predictions rather than analysis of the outcomes. Considering everything, some assumptions could be broken if the designed model is stable and has high performance.

- **"Binary Output Variable":** This may be evident as we have already discussed it earlier, but "logistic regression" is designed specifically for issues with "binary (two-class) classification". This will generate predictions for the probability of a default class instance that can be tagged into a classification of "0" or "1".

- **"Remove Noise":** Logistic regression does not assume errors in the "output variable ('y')", therefore, the "outliers and potentially misclassified" cases should be removed from the training data set.

- **"Gaussian Distribution":** Logistic regression can be considered as a type of "linear algorithm but with a non-linear transform on the output". A liner connection between the output and input variables is also assumed. Data transformations of the input variables may lead to a more accurate model with a higher capability of revealing the linear relationships of the data set. For instance, to better reveal these relationships, we could utilize "log", "root", "Box-Cox" and other single variable transformations.

- **"Remove Correlated Inputs":** If you have various highly correlated inputs, the model could potentially be "over-fit" similar the "linear regression" technique. To address this issue, you can "calculate the pairwise correlations between all input data points and remove the highly correlated inputs".

- **"Failure to converge":** It is likely for the "expected likelihood estimation" method that is trained on the coefficients that have failed to converge. It could occur if the data set contains several highly correlated inputs, or there is a very limited data (e.g. loads of "0" in the input).

"Naïve Bayes classifier algorithm" is another "classification" learning algorithm with a wide variety of applications. It is a method of classification derived from the "Bayes theorem", which assumes predictors are independent of one another. The "Naïve Bayes classifier" will assume that "all the features in a class are unrelated to the existence of any other feature in that class". For instance, if input data has an image of a fruit that is green, round, and about 10 inches in diameter, the model can consider the input to be a watermelon. Although these attributes rely on one another or on the presence of a specific feature, all of the characteristics contribute freely to the probability that the image of the fruit is that of a watermelon, hence it is referred to as "Naive". "Naïve Bayes model" for large volumes of datasets is relatively easy to construct and extremely effective.

"Naïve Bayes" has reportedly outperformed even the most sophisticated techniques of classification, even considering the easy of its development. "Bayes theorem" can also provide the means to calculate the posterior probability "P(c|x)" using "P(c), P(x), and P(x)". On the basis of the equation shown in the picture below, where the probability of "c" can be calculated if "x" has already occurred.

"P(c|x)" is the posterior probability of "class (c, target)" provided by the "predictor (x, attributes)". "P(c)" is the class's previous probability. "P(x|c)" is the probability of the class provided by the predictor. "P(x)" is the predictor's prior probability.

$$P(c \mid x) = \frac{P(x \mid c)\, P(c)}{P(x)}$$

Likelihood

Class Prior Probability

Posterior Probability

Predictor Prior Probability

$$P(c \mid X) = P(x_1 \mid c) \times P(x_2 \mid c) \times \cdots \times P(x_n \mid c) \times P(c)$$

Here is an example to better explain the application of the "Bayes Theorem". The picture below represents the data set pertaining to the problem of identifying suitable weather days to play golf. The columns depict the weather features of the day and the rows contain individual entries. Considering the first row of the data set, it can be concluded that the weather will be too hot and humid with rain so the day is not suitable to play golf. Now, the primary assumption here is that all these features or predictors are independent of one another. The other assumption being made here is that all the predictors have potentially the same effect on the end result. Meaning, if the day was windy, it would have some relevance to the decision of playing golf as the rain. In this example, the variable (c) is the class (playing golf) representing the decision if the weather is suitable for golf and variable (x) represents the features or predictors.

	OUTLOOK	TEMPERATURE	HUMIDITY	WINDY	PLAY GOLF
0	Rainy	Hot	High	False	No
1	Rainy	Hot	High	True	No
2	Overcast	Hot	High	False	Yes
3	Sunny	Mild	High	False	Yes
4	Sunny	Cool	Normal	False	Yes
5	Sunny	Cool	Normal	True	No
6	Overcast	Cool	Normal	True	Yes

7	Rainy	Mild	High	False	No
8	Rainy	Cool	Normal	False	Yes
9	Sunny	Mild	Normal	False	Yes
10	Rainy	Mild	Normal	True	Yes
11	Overcast	Mild	High	True	Yes
12	Overcast	Hot	Normal	False	Yes
13	Sunny	Mild	High	True	No

Types of "Naïve Bayes classifier".

- **"Multinomial Naïve Bayes"** - This is widely used to classify documents, for example, which category does a document belong: beauty, technology, politics, and so on. The frequency of the phrases in the document is considered as the features or predictors of the classifier.

- **"Bernoulli Naive Bayes"** - This is nearly identical to the "Multinomial Naïve Bayes", however, the predictors used here are the "boolean variables". For example, depending on whether a select phrase occurs in the text or not, the parameters used to predict the class variable can either be a yes or no value.

- **"Gaussian Naive Bayes"** - When the predictors are not distinct and have very similar or continuous values, it can be assumed that these values are obtained from a Gaussian distribution.

Applications of "Naïve Bayes"

- **Real-Time Prediction"**: Naive Bayes is extremely quick in learning from the input data and can be seamlessly used to generate real-time predictions.

- **"Multi-class Prediction"**: This algorithm is widely used to generate predictions for multiple classes at the same time. It allows the prediction of the probability of various classes of the target variable.

- **"Text classification / Spam Filtering / Sentiment Analysis"**: The "Naive Bayes classifiers" is heavily utilized in text classification models owing to its ability to address problems with multiple classes of the target variable and the rule of autonomy. This algorithm has reported higher success rates than any other algorithm. As a consequence, it is commonly used for the identification of spam emails and sentiment analysis by identifying favorable and negative consumer feelings on the social media platforms.

- **"Recommendation System"**: "Naive Bayes Classifier" and "Collaborative Filtering" can be combined together to generate a this system that utilizes ML and data mining methods to filter hidden data and generate insight as to whether the customer would prefer a particular item or product.

Ensemble Methods

Imagine that you've chosen to construct a car because you're not pleased with the variety of cars available in stores and online. You may start by discovering the best option for each component that you need. The resulting car will outshine all the other alternatives with the assembly of all these excellent components. Ensemble methods use the same concept of mixing several predictive models (controlled ML) to obtain results of greater quality than any of the models could provide on their own. The "Random Forest" algorithms, for instance, is an ensemble technique that combines many trained "Decision Trees" with various data sets samples. As a result, the quality of predictions generated by "Random Forest" method is higher than the quality of the estimated predictions with a single "Decision Tree".

Think of ensemble methods as an approach for reducing a single machine learning model's variance and bias. This is essential because, under certain circumstances, any specified model may be accurate but completely incorrect under other circumstances. The relative accuracy could be overturned with another model. The quality of the predictions is balanced by merging the two models.

Decision Trees

To refresh your memory, a machine learning decision tree can be defined as "a tree like graphical representation of the decision making process by taking into consideration all the conditions or factors that can influence the decision and the consequences of those decisions". Decision trees are considered one of the simplest "supervised machine learning algorithms" and have three main elements: "branch nodes" representing conditions of the data set, "edges" representing ongoing decision process and "leaf nodes" representing the end of the decision. There are two types of decision trees: "Classification tree" that is used to classify Data for information on the basis of existing system data available in the system; "Regression tree", which is used to make a forecast for predictions for future events on the basis of existing system data. Both of these trees are heavily used in machine learning algorithms. A widely used terminology for decision trees is "Classification and Regression trees" or "CART".

Support vector machine learning algorithm (SVM)

This is a type of "supervised machine learning algorithm", used for "classification" or "regression", wherein the dataset teaches SVM about classes to allow classification of any new data. It operates by classifying the data into various classes by discovering a line (hyper-plane) that divides the collection of training data into classes. Due to the availability of various linear hyper-planes, this algorithm attempts to maximize the distance between the different classes involved, which is known as "margin maximization". By identifying the line that maximizes the class distance, the likelihood of generalizing apparent to unseen data can be improved.

SVM's can be categorized into two as follows:

- "Linear SVM's" – In linear SVM's, the training data or classifiers can be divided by a hyper-plane.
- "Non-Linear SVM's" – Unlike linear SVMs, in non-linear SVM's the possibility to separate the training data with a hyper-plane does not exist. For example, the Face Detection training data consists of a group of facial images and another group of non-facial images. The training data is highly complicated under such circumstances that it is difficult to discover a representation for each feature vector. It is extremely complex to separate the set of faces linearly from the set of non-facial data.

SVM is widely used by different economic organizations for stock market forecasting. For example, SVM may be utilized for comparison of relative stock performances, in comparison to the performances of other stocks within an industrial sector. Relative stock comparisons help in the investments related decision making process, on the basis of the classifications generated by SVM algorithms.

The Kernel Trick
The data collected in the real world is randomly distributed and making it too difficult to separate different classes linearly. However, if one can potentially figure out a way for mapping the data from 2-D space to 3-D space, as shown in the picture below, they would be

able to discover a decision surface that obviously separates distinct classes.

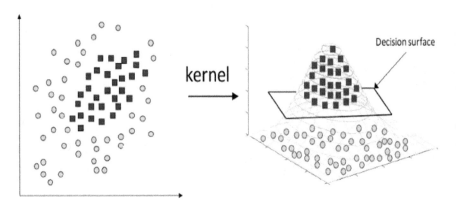

One approach to transforming data like this is mapping all data points to a higher dimension (for this example, it is 3 dimensions), finding the limit, and making the classifications. That works for a limited number of dimensions but computations within a given space becomes increasingly costly when there are a lot of dimensions to deal with. And so the kernel trick comes to the rescue! The "kernel trick" enables us to function in the original feature space without needing to calculate the data coordinates in a higher dimensional space. For example, the equation in the picture below has a couple of 3-D data points as 'x' and 'y.'

$$\mathbf{x} = (x_1, x_2, x_3)^T$$
$$\mathbf{y} = (y_1, y_2, y_3)^T$$

Suppose we want to map "x" and "y" to 9-D space. To get the final outcome, which would be just scalar, we have to do the calculations shown in the picture below. In this case, the computational complexity will be O(n2).

$$\phi(\mathbf{x}) = \left(x_1^2, x_1x_2, x_1x_3, x_2x_1, x_2^2, x_2x_3, x_3x_1, x_3x_2, x_3^2\right)^T$$
$$\phi(\mathbf{y}) = \left(y_1^2, y_1y_2, y_1y_3, y_2y_1, y_2^2, y_2y_3, y_3y_1, y_3y_2, y_3^2\right)^T$$

$$\phi(\mathbf{x})^T \phi(\mathbf{y}) = \sum_{i,j=1}^{3} x_i x_j y_i y_j$$

However, by using the "kernel function", indicated as "k(x, y)", in lieu of performing the complex calculations in the 9-D space, the same outcome can be achieved in the 3-D space with calculation of the "dot product" of 'x-transpose' and 'y.' In this case, the complex computations will be "O(n)".

$$
\begin{aligned}
k(\mathbf{x}, \mathbf{y}) &= (\mathbf{x}^T \mathbf{y})^2 \\
&= (x_1 y_1 + x_2 y_2 + x_3 y_3)^2 \\
&= \sum_{i,j=1}^{3} x_i x_j y_i y_j
\end{aligned}
$$

In principle, this trick is used to make the transformation of data into higher dimensions much more effective and less costly. The use of this trick is not restricted to the SVM algorithm and can be utilized with any computations that involve the "dot products (x, y)".

Review Quiz

Answer the questions below to verify your understanding of the concepts explained in this chapter. The answer key can be found at the end of the quiz.

1.   What are the different types of machine learning algorithms?

2.   Name the type of algorithm that is widely used for predictive data analysis.

3.   Name the type of algorithm that are capable of utilizing raw data just as well as the labeled data.

4.   What are the 2 features that are unique to Reinforcement algorithms?

5. ____ is one of the supervised algorithms that can be trained with multiple by calculating a line's position and slope.

6. ____ is another supervised algorithm that can generate predictions or explanations for a class value.

7. Define Naïve Bayes classifier algorithm.

8. The most popular algorithm used by different economic organizations for stock market forecasting.

Answer Key

1. Supervised, Unsupervised, Semi-supervised, Reinforcement

2. Supervised machine learning algorithms

3. Semi-supervised machine learning algorithms

4. Trial and error research method, Delayed reward feedback loop

5. Linear regression

6. Classification

7. It is a method of classification derived from the Bayes theorem, which assumes predictors are independent of one another.

8. Support vector machine learning algorithm

Day 4: Unsupervised Machine Learning Algorithms

Working with a large volume of raw and unstructured data can be very challenging. Companies frequently run into issues of not being able to access the required information from the source, which prevents them from generating a labeled and classified training data set to develop the desired machine learning model. This is where the unsupervised machine learning algorithms come to the rescue. Unsupervised ML algorithms have a wide array of usage in defining how the machines can generate "inferred features" for the elucidation of a concealed construct from the stack of unlabeled and unclassified data collection. These algorithms are capable of exploring the data in order to define a structure within the data mass. Unlike the supervised machine learning algorithms, unsupervised algorithms are unable to identify the correct output, even though they have similar efficacy as the supervised learning algorithms in investigating input data and drawing inferences. These algorithms can be used to identify information outliers, generate tailored and custom product recommendations, classify text subjects by utilizing methods such as "self-organizing maps", "singular value decomposition" and "k-means clustering". For instance, these algorithms are being utilized to identify customers with shared shopping characteristics which are then segmented into specific groups with a singular focus based marketing strategies and campaigns. As a result, the online marketing world is heavily dependent on unsupervised learning algorithms.

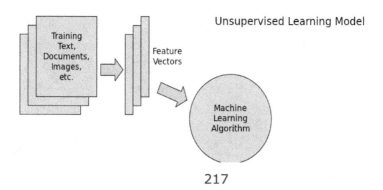

217

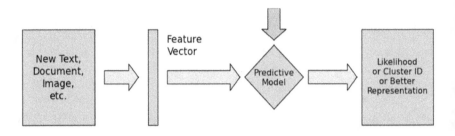

Some of the most widely used unsupervised algorithms are described below:

Clustering

We enter the category of unsupervised machine learning, with "clustering methods" because its objective is to "group or cluster observations with comparable features". Clustering methods do not use output data to train but allow the output to be defined by the algorithm. Only data visualizations can be used in clustering techniques to check the solution's quality. "K-Means clustering", where 'K' is used to represent the no. of "clusters" that the customer elects to generate a machine learning model and is the most common clustering method. (Note that different methods for selecting K value, such as the "elbow technique" are also available.)

Steps used by K-Means clustering to process the data points:

1.   The data centers are selected randomly by 'K.'

2.   Assigns each data point to the nearest centers that have been randomly generated.

3.   Re-calculates each cluster's center.

4.   If centers do not change (or have minor change), the process will be completed.

Otherwise, we'll go back to step 2. (Set a maximum amount of iterations in advance to avoid getting stuck in an infinite loop, if the center of the cluster continues to alter.)

The following plot applies "K-Means" to a building data set. Each column in the plot shows each building's efficiency. The four measurements relate to air conditioning, heating, installed electronic appliances (refrigerators, TV), and cooking gas. For simplicity of interpretation of the results, 'K' can be set to value '2' for clustering, wherein one cluster will be selected as an efficient building group and the other cluster as an inefficient building group. You see the place of the structures on the left as well as a couple of the building characteristics used as inputs on the right: installed electronic appliances and heating.

Dimensionality Reduction

As the name indicates, to extract the least significant information (sometimes redundant columns) from a data set, we use "dimensionality reduction". In practice, data sets tend to contain hundreds and thousands of rows (also known as characteristics), which makes it essential to decrease the total number of rows. For example, pictures may contain thousands of pixels; all those pixels are not important for the analysis. Or a large number of measurements or experiments can be applied to every single chip while testing microchips within the manufacturing process, the majority of which produce redundant data. In such scenarios, "dimensionality reduction" algorithms are leveraged to manage the data set.

Principal Component Analysis (PCA)

It is the most common "dimension reduction technique", which reduces the size of the "feature space" by discovering new vectors that are capable of maximizing the linear variety of the data. When the linear correlations of the data are powerful, PCA can dramatically reduce the data dimension while maintaining most of the information. PCA is one of the fundamental ML algorithms. It enables you to reduce the data dimension, losing as little info as possible. It is used in many fields such as object recognition, the vision of computers, compression of information, etc. The calculation of the main parts is limited to the calculation of the initial data's own vectors and covariance matrix values or to the data matrix's unique decomposition. Through one, we can convey several indications, merge, so to speak, and operate with a simpler model already. Of course, most probably, data loss will not be avoided, but the PCA technique will assist us to minimize any losses.

t-Stochastic Neighbor Embedding (t-SNE)

Another common technique is "t-Stochastic Neighbor Embedding (t-SNE)", which results in a decrease of non-linear dimensionality. This technique is primarily used for data visualization, with potential use for machine learning functions such as space reduction and clustering. The next plot demonstrates "MNIST database" analysis of handwritten digits. "MNIST" includes a large number of digit pictures from 0 to 9, used by scientists to test "clustering" and "classification" algorithms. Individual row of the data set represents "vectorized version" of the original picture (size 28x28 = 784 pixels) and a label (0, 1, 2, and so on) for each picture. Note that the dimensionality is therefore reduced from 784 pixels to 2-D in the plot below. Two-dimensional projecting enables visualization of the initial high-dimensional data set.

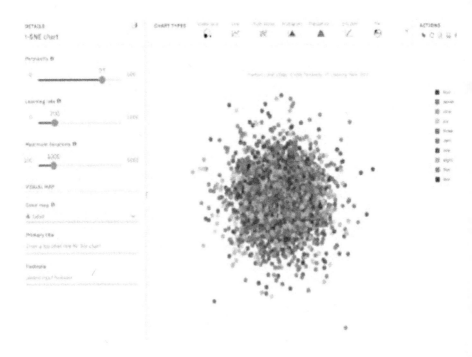

Transfer Learning

Imagine you are a data scientist focusing on the clothing industry. You have been training a high-quality learning model for months to be able to classify pictures of "women's tops" as tops, tank tops, and blouses. You have been tasked to create a comparable model for classification of pants pictures such as jeans, trousers and chinos. With the use of the "Transfer Learning" method, the understanding incorporated into the first model be seamlessly transferred and applied to the second model.

Transfer Learning pertains to the re-use and adaptation of a portion of a previously trained neural network to a fresh but comparable assignment. Specifically, once a neural network has been successfully trained for a particular task, a proportion of the trained layers can be easily transferred and combined with new layers that are then trained on pertinent data for the new task. This new "neural network" can learn and adapt rapidly to the new assignment by incorporating a few layers.

The primary benefit of transferring learning is a decrease in the volume of data required to train the neural network resulting in cost savings for the development of "deep learning algorithms". Not to forget how hard it can be to even procure a sufficient amount of labeled data required for training the model. Suppose in this example; you are utilizing a neural network with 20 hidden layers for the "women's top" model. You understand after running a few tests that 16 of the women's top model layers can be transferred and combined them with new set of data to train on pants pictures. Therefore, the new pants model will have 17 concealed layers. The input and output of both the tasks are distinct, but the reusable layers are capable of summarizing the data appropriate to both, e.g. clothing, zippers, and shape of the garment.

Transfer learning is getting increasingly popular, so much so that for basic "deep learning tasks" such as picture and text classification, a variety of high quality pre-trained models are already available in the market.

Natural Language Processing

A majority of the knowledge and information pertaining to our world is in some type of human language. Once deemed as impossible to achieve, today, computers are capable of reading large volumes of books and blogs within minutes. Although computers are still unable to fully comprehend "human text", but they can be trained to perform specific tasks. Mobile devices, for instance, can be trained to auto-complete text messages or fix spelling mistakes. Machines have been trained enough to hold straightforward conversations like humans. "Natural Language Processing" (NLP) is not exactly a method of ML, instead it is a commonly used technique to produce texts for machine learning. Consider multitude of formats of tons of text files (words, internet blogs etc.). Most of these text files are usually flooded with typing errors, grammatically incorrect characters and phrases that need to be filtered out. The most popular text processing model available in the market today is "NLTK (Natural Language ToolKit)", developed by "Stanford University" researchers.

The easiest approach to map texts into numerical representations is calculation of the frequency of each word contained in every text document. For example, an integer matrix where individual rows represent one text document and every column represents single word. This word frequency representation matrix is frequently referred to as the "Term Frequency Matrix" (TFM). From there, individual matrix entries can be separated by a weight of how essential every single term is within the whole stack of papers. This form of matrix representations of text documents is called as "Term Frequency Inverse Document Frequency" (TFIDF), which usually yields better performance for machine learning tasks.

Word Embedding

"Term Frequency Matrix" and "Term Frequency Inverse Document Frequency" are numerical representations of text papers which only take into account frequency and weighted frequencies to represent text files. On the other hand, "Word Embedding" in a document is capable of capturing the actual context of a word. Embedding can quantify the similarity between phrases within the context of the word, which subsequently allows execution of arithmetic operations with words. "Word2Vec" is a neural network based technique that can map phrases to a numerical vector in a corpus. These vectors are then used to discover synonyms, do arithmetic with words or phrases, or to represent text files. Let's suppose, for instance, a large enough body of text files was used to estimate word embedding. Suppose the words "king, queen, man and female" are found in the corpus and vector ("word") is the number vector representing the word "word". We can conduct arithmetic procedure with numbers to estimate vector('woman'):

$vector('king')$ + $vector('woman') - vector('man')$ ~ $vector('queen')$

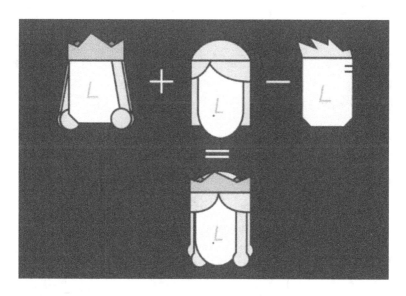

Word depictions enable similarities to be found between phrases by calculating the "cosine similarity" between the vector representation of the two words. The "cosine similarity" gives a measure of the angle between two vectors. We use machine learning techniques to calculate word embedding, but this is often a preliminary step in implementing a machine learning algorithm on top of the word embedding method. For example, the "Twitter" user database containing large volume of "tweets" can be leveraged to understand which of these customers purchased a house recently. We can merge "Word2Vec" with a logistic regression to generate predictions on the likelihood of a new "Twitter" user purchasing a home.

Apriori machine learning algorithm

"Apriori algorithm" is another unsupervised ML algorithm that can produce rules of association from a specified set of data. "Association rule" simply means if an item X exists then the item Y has a predefined probability of existence. Most rules of association are produced in the format of "IF-THEN" statements. For instance, "IF" someone purchases an iPhone, "THEN" they have most likely purchased an iPhone case as well. The Apriori algorithm is able to draw these findings by initially observing the number of individuals who purchased an iPhone case while making an iPhone purchase and generating a ratio obtained by dividing the number individuals who bought a new iPhone (1000) with individuals who also bought an iPhone case (800) with their new iPhones. The fundamental principles of Apriori ML Algorithm are:

- If a set of events have high frequency of occurrence, then all subsets of that event set will also have high frequency of occurrence.
- If a set of events occur occasionally, then all supersets of the event set of will occur occasionally as well.

Apriori algorithm has wide applicability in following areas:

"Detecting Adverse Drug Reactions"

"Apriori algorithm" is used to analyze healthcare data such as the drugs administered to the patient, characteristics of each patient, harmful side effects experienced by the patient, the original diagnosis, among others. This analysis generates rules of association that provide insight on the characteristic of the patient and the administered drug that potentially contributed to harmful side-effects of the drug.

"Market Basket Analysis"

Some of the leading online e-commerce businesses including "Amazon", use Apriori algorithm to gather insights on products that have high likelihood of being bought together and products that can have an upsell with product promotions and discount offers. For instance, Apriori could be used by a retailer to generate prediction such as: customers purchasing sugar and flour have high likelihood of purchasing eggs to bake cookies and cakes.

"Auto-Complete Applications"

The highly cherished auto-complete feature on "Google" is another common Apriori application. When the user starts typing in their keywords for a search, the search engine searches its database, for other related phrases that are usually typed in after a particular word.

Review Quiz

Answer the questions below to verify your understanding of the concepts explained in this chapter. The answer key can be found at the end of the quiz.

1.   ____ algorithms can be used to define how the machines can generate inferred from raw data.

2.   How are the machines trained with the use of the clustering method?

3.   Name the method used to represent the number of clusters elected by the customer to generate a machine learning model.

4.   What algorithm is used for extraction of the least significant information or redundant columns from a data set.

5.   Which dimensionality reduction technique may be utilized to reduce the size of the feature space by maximizing the linear variety of the data?

6.   Which dimensionality reduction technique may be utilized to reduce the non-linearity of the data?

7.   Define the transfer learning method.

8.   Name the technique used to produce text based data for machine learning models such as auto-complete feature on mobile messaging applications.

Answer Key

1.   Unsupervised

2.   Clustering methods use output data to train but allow the output to be defined by the algorithm on the basis of group observations generated on comparable features.

3.   K-means clustering

4.   Dimensionality reduction

5.   Principal Component Analysis

6.   t-Stochastic Neighbor Embedding

7.   The reuse and adaptation of portion of a previously trained neural network to a fresh but comparable assignment is defined as transfer learning.

8.   Natural Language Processing

Day 5: Data Pre-processing and Creation of Training Dataset

Data Preprocessing is a "data mining technique, which is used to transform raw data into a comprehensible and effective format". Real-world data tends to lack certain behaviors or trends and is almost always incomplete, inconsistent, and/or missing attribute values, flooded with errors or outliers.

Preprocessing data is a proven way to solve such problems. This raw data or real data from the world cannot be readily transmitted through a machine learning model. Therefore, before feeding real world data to a machine learning model, we need to clean and pre-process it.

Overview Data Preprocessing

Data Cleaning:
Many meaningless and missing sections can be found in the data. "Data cleaning" is performed in order to manage these inadequacies and constitutes handling data set that is missing values and consists of noisy data.

Missing Data
In this scenario, certain significant information in the data set is missing. It can be dealt with in different respects, such as:

- **Ignoring the tuples:** This strategy is appropriate only if the dataset is big, and numerous values within a tuple are lacking.

- **Fill the missing values:** This assignment can be done in different ways, such as: manually completing the missing values by utilizing the mean attribute or the most relevant value.

Noisy Data

"Noisy data" is useless data that machines or the machine learning model is unable to interpret. It can be generated as a result of defective data collection or mistakes in data entry, among others. It can be addressed by utilizing the methods below:

- **Binning Method:** This technique operates on sorted data to smoothen it out. The entire data set is split into equivalent size sections, and then different techniques are used to finish the job. Each section is fixed individually. To fix the entire data set in ago, all data points in a section can be substituted with its "mean" or most probable values.

- **Regression:** In this case, data may be smoothened by fitting into a "regression function", which can be either "linear" (with one autonomous variable) or "multiple" (with various autonomous variables).

- **Clustering:** This technique is used to group comparable data points into a cluster. The outliers could be obtained with data points falling outside of the clusters or could not be detected.

Data Transformation

This technique is used to convert the data into format, which is suitable for the data mining method. This includes the following ways:

- **Normalization:** This technique is used to scale data values within a defined range, for example, "-1.0 to 1.0" or "0.0 to 1.0".

- **Attribute Selection:** New data attributes can be generated from the existing data set of characteristics by utilizing this technique to assist in the data mining process.

- **Discretization:** This technique is used to "replace raw values of numerical attributes with interval or conceptual levels".

- **Generation of the concept of hierarchy:** This technique is used to transform lower level data attributes to higher level in the hierarchical set up. For example, you can convert the attribute "city" to "country".

Data Reduction

"Data mining" is a method used for analysis and extraction of insights from Big data. In such instances, analysis becomes more and more difficult to work with, given the enormity of data. We use data reduction method to decrease the volume of data set to an optimal and manageable volume. With this method the cost of data storage and analysis can be significantly lowered while improving the effectiveness of the data storage. It can be dealt with in different respects such as:

- **Data Cube Aggregation:** This technique is used to apply "aggregation operation" to data to effectively build data cubes.

- **Selection of attribute subset:** This technique is used to ensure that only necessary data attributes are used, and the not so relevant attributes can be discarded. To perform attribute selection, the "level of significance" and "p-value of the attribute" can be leveraged. The attribute with "p-value" higher than the "significance level" can be removed to obtain optimal volume of the data set.

- **Numerosity Reduction:** This technique allows the data model to be stored instead of the whole data set or raw data collected from various input sources, for instance, "Regression Models".

Dimensionality Reduction: This technique uses encoding mechanisms to reduce the volume of the data set. If initial data set can be recovered after reconstruction from compressed data set, this reduction in dimensions of the dataset is called as "lossless reduction", otherwise, it is referred to as "loss reduction".

The two efficient techniques of reducing data set "dimensionality" are: "Wavelet transforms" and "PCA (Principal Component Analysis)".

Steps of Data Pre-processing

I – Import the data library

There is a wide variety of data libraries available that you can choose to meet your data requirements, such as:

"Pandas": Widely used for data visualization and data manipulation processes.
"NumPy": A basic package to perform scientific computations with the use of Python programming language.
"Matplotlib": A standard Python Library used by data scientists to create 2-D plots and graphs.
"Seaborn": Seaborn is derived from the "Matplotlib" library and an extremely popular visualization library.

For example, you can use the main libraries from "Pandas", "NumPy" and "time"; data visualization libraries from "Matplotlib" and "Seaborn"; and Scikit-Learn libraries for the data preprocessing techniques and algorithms.To import the libraries mentioned above, use the code below:

For main libraries *"import pandas as pd import numpy as np import time"*
For visualization libraries *"from matplotlib import pyplot as plt import seaborn as sns from mpl_toolkits.mplot3d import Axes3D plt.style.use('ggplot')"*
For Scikit-Learn libraries *"from sklearn.neighbors import KNeighborsClassifier from sklearn.model_selection import*

train_test_split from sklearn.preprocessing import normalize from sklearn.metrics import confusion_matrix,accuracy_score,precision_score,recall_score,f1_scor e,matthews_corrcoef,classification_report,roc_curve from sklearn.externals import joblib from sklearn.preprocessing import StandardScaler from sklearn.decomposition import PCA"

II – Data exploration

To get some sense of the imported dataset in Pandas, use the code below:

"# Read the data in the CSV file using pandas df = pd.read_csv('../input/creditcard.csv') df.head()"

III – Check for missing values

It is essential to comprehend the concept of missing values to be able to effectively manage data. If the researcher does not handle the missing values correctly, they may end up drawing incorrect data inferences. Because of improper handling, the results produced will be different from those with missing values. You can apply any of the techniques below to deal with missing data values in your data set:

1. Ignoring the data row

It's generally performed when the "class label" is missing or if multiple data attribute are missing in the row, assuming the data mining objective is classification. However, if the proportion of such rows with missing class labels is high, you will obviously get bad output. For instance, database with enrolment data for the student (age, SAT score, address, etc.) containing a column with "Low", "Medium" and "High" to classify their achievement in college. Assuming the objective is to construct a model that predicts the college achievement of a student. Data rows that do not include the achievement column are not helpful to generate predictions regarding the success of the student, so they can be overlooked and deleted before the algorithm is executed.

2. Using a global constant for filling in the missing values

In this technique, an appropriate and new global constant value is selected, such as "unknown", "N / A" or "minus infinity", which is then utilized for filling all the missing values. This method is employed when the concerted effort to predict the missing value just doesn't make sense. Let's consider the student enrollment database example again, assume that some students lack information on the 'state of residence' attribute. It doesn't really make sense to fill it with some random state instead of using "N/A".

3. Using attribute mean

This technique is used to replace an attribute's missing values with the "mean or median value (if its discrete)" for specific attribute in the database. For instance, in a US family expenditure database, if the average expenses of a family are A then we may be able to utilize A to replace missing values in the other family records.

4. Using attribute mean for all samples belonging to the same class

This technique is used to restrict the calculations to a particular class for obtaining a value that is applicable to the row that we are searching for in lieu of utilizing the "mean (or medians)" of a particular attribute calculated by searching all the rows of the database. For example, if you have an automobile price database that classifies vehicles, among other things, into "Luxury" and "Low Budget". It is likely more precise to replace the missing price of a "luxury car" with the average price of all luxury vehicles instead of the value obtained after factoring in "low budget cars".

5. Using data mining algorithm for prediction of the most probable value

Data mining algorithms such as "Regression", inference based tools utilizing the Bayesian formula, "decision trees", clustering algorithms (K-Mean or Median) among others, can be used to determine the probable value of the data attribute. For instance, "clustering algorithms" could be employed to produce a cluster of rows that are then used to calculate the mean or median of the attribute, as indicated earlier in Technique 3. Another instance might be to use a decision tree to generate a prediction for the most probable value of the missing attributes by taking into account all other attributes in the data set.

IV – Dealing with Categorical Data values

Categorical attributes can only take on a restricted amount of feasible values, which are generally fixed. For instance, if a dataset is about user-related data, then characteristics such as 'nation,' 'gender,' 'age group,' etc. will constitute the data set. Alternatively, you will find attributes such as 'product type,' 'manufacturer,' 'vendor,' and so on if your data set pertains to a commodity or product.

In context of the data set, these are all categorical attributes. Typically, these attributes are stored as text values representing different characteristics of the observations. Gender is defined, for instance, as "male" or "female", and product type could be defined as "electronics", "apparel", "food", and so on.

There are three types of categorical data:

- **Nominal** – The types of attributes where categories are only labeled and have no order of succession are called "nominal features". For example, gender could be 'male' (M) or 'female' (F) and have no order of precedence.

- **Ordinal** – The types of attributes where categories are labeled with an order of precedence are called "ordinal features". For example, an economic status feature can contain three categories: "low", "medium", and "high", which have an inherent order associated with them.

- **Continuous** – The types of attributes where categories are numerical variables with infinite values ranging between two defined values are called "continuous features".

Challenges of Categorical Data:

- Categorical attributes can contain multiple levels, called as "high cardinality" (e.g. states, towns or URLs), where most levels appear in relatively smaller number of instances.

- Various ML models are algebraic, such as "regression" and "SVM", which require numerical input. Categories have to be changed first to numbers in order to use these models before the machine learning algorithm can be applied.

- While some machine learning packages or libraries are capable of automatically transforming the categorical data into numeric, depending on the default embedded technique, a variety of machine learning libraries don't support categorical data inputs.

- Categorical data for the computer does not translate the context or background, that people can readily associate with and comprehend. For instance, consider a function called "City" with different city names like "New York", "New Jersey", and "New Delhi". People know that "New York" is strongly linked to "New Jersey" being two neighboring states of America, while "New York" and "New Delhi" are very distinct. On the other hand, for the machine, all three cities just denote three distinct levels of the same "City" function. Without specifying adequate context through data for the model, differentiating between extremely distinct levels will be difficult for it.

Encoding Categorical Data:

ML models are built on math equations, so it is easy to comprehend that maintaining the categorical data in equations would cause issues since equations are primarily driven by numbers alone.

To cross this hurdle, the categorical features can be encoded to numeric quantities. The encoding techniques below will be described with the use of the example of an "airline carrier" column from a make believe airline database, for ease of understanding. However, it is possible to extend the same techniques to any desired column.

1.   Replacing the categorical values

This is a fundamental technique of replacing the categorical data values with required integers. The *"replace()"* function in Pandas, can be used for this technique. Depending on your business requirements, desired numbers can be easily assigned to the categorical values.

2.   Encoding Labels

The technique of converting categorical values in a column to a number is called as "label encoding". Numerical labels always range from "0" to "n categories-1". Encoding a group of category to a certain numerical value and then encoding all other categories to another numerical value can be done by utilizing the *"where()"* function in NumPy. For example, one could encode all the "US airline carriers" to value "1" and all other carriers can be given a value "0". You can perform similar label encoding by utilizing the Scikit-Learn Label Encoder.

Label encoding is fairly intuitive and simple and produce satisfactory performance from your learning algorithm. However, the algorithm is at a disadvantage and may misinterpret numerical values. For example, algorithm may confuse whether the "U.S. airline carrier" (encoded to 6) should be given 6 times more weight "U.S. airline carrier" (encoded to 1).

3.   One-Hot encoding

To resolve the misinterpretation issue of the machine learning algorithm generated by the "label encoding" technique, each categorical data value can be transformed into a new column, and that new column can be allocated a '1' or '0' (True/False) value, and is called as "one-hot encoding".

Of all the machine learning libraries in the market that offer "one-hot encoding", the easiest one is *get_dummies()* technique in "Pandas", which is appropriately titled given the fact that dummy/indicator data variables such as "1" or "0" are created. In its preprocessing module, Scikit-Learn also supports "one-hot encoding" in it's pre-processing module via "LabelBinarizer" and "OneHotEncoder" techniques.

While "one-hot encoding" addresses the issue of misinterpreted category weights, it gives rise to another issue. Creation of multiple new columns to solve this category weight problem for numerous categories can lead to a "curse of dimensionality". The logic behind "curse of dimensionality" is that some equations simply stop functioning correctly in high-dimensional spaces.

4.   Binary encoding

This method initially encodes the categories as "ordinal", then converts these integers into a binary string, and then divides digits of that binary code into distinct columns. Therefore, the data is encoded in only a few dimensions unlike the "one-hot encoding" method.

There are several options to implement binary encoding in your machine learning model, but the easiest option is to install "category_encoders" library. This can be done with the use of the "pip install category_encoders" file on cmd.

Backward difference encoding

This "backward difference encoding" method falls within the "contrast coding scheme" for categorical attributes. A "K" category or level characteristic typically enters a "regression" as a series of dummy "K-1" variables. This technique works by drawing a comparison between the "mean" of the dependent variable for a level with the "mean" of the dependent variable in the preceding stage. This kind of encoding is widely used for a "nominal" or an "ordinal "variable".

The code structure for this technique is quite similar to any other technique in the "category_encoders" library, except the run command for this technique is "BackwardDifferenceEncoder".

5. Miscellaneous features

You may sometimes deal with categorical columns that indicate the range of values in observation points; for instance, an 'age' column can contain categories such as '0-20', '20-40', '40-60' etc. While there may be many methods to handle such attributes, the most popular ones are:

A. Dividing the categorical value ranges into two distinct columns, by first creating a dummy data frame with just one feature as "age" and then splitting the column on the delimiter "(-)" into two columns "start" and "end" using "split()" and "lambda()" functions .

B. Replacing the categorical value ranges with select measure like the mean value of the range, by utilizing the "split_mean()" function.

V – Splitting the data set into Training and Testing data subsets

The ML algorithms are required to learn from sample data set to be able to generate predictions from the input data set. In general, we divide the data set into a proportion of 65:35 or 80:20, which means that 65% of the data is utilized as the training subset, and 35% of the data is utilized as the testing subset. However, this split ratio is adjusted according to the form and size of the data set.

It is almost impossible and futile to manually split the data set while making sure the data set is divided randomly. The Scikit-Learn library offers us a tool called the "Model Selection library" to assist with this task. There is a class in the Scikit-Learn library called "train_test_split". With the use of this class, we can readily divide the data set into the "training" and "testing" datasets in desired ratios. Certain important parameters that should be considered with the use of this tool are:

- **Test_size** - It helps in determining the size of the data to be divided as the testing data set, as a fraction of the total data set. For example, entering 0.3 as the "test_size" value, the data set will be divided at 30 percent as the test data set. If you specify this parameter, the next parameter may be ignored.

- **Train_size** – This parameter is only specified if the "test_size" has not been specified already. The process works similar to the "test_size" function, except that the percentage of the data set specified is for the "training set".

- **Random_state** - An integer is entered here for the Scikit-Learn class, on the basis of which the "random number generator" will be activated during the data set split. Alternatively, an instance of "RandomState" class can b entered that will then generate random numbers. If you don't enter either of the functions, the default will be activated, which leverages the "RandomState" instance used by "np.random".

For example, the data set in the picture below can be split into two subsets: 'X' subset for the "independent features" and 'Y' subset for the "dependent variables" and also happens to be the last column of the data set.

Country	Age	Salary	Purchased
France	44	72000	No
Spain	27	48000	Yes
Germany	30	54000	No
Spain	38	61000	No
Germany	40	nan	Yes
France	35	58000	Yes
Spain	nan	52000	No
France	48	79000	Yes
Germany	50	83000	No
France	37	67000	Yes

Now we can use the code below for splitting the "x" data set into two subsets: "xTrain" and "xTest" and likewise, divide the "y" data set into two subsets "yTrain" and "yTest".

"from sklearn.model_selection import train_test_split xTrain, xTest, yTrain, yTest = train_test_split (x, y, test_size = 0.2, random_state = 0)"

According to the code above, the test data set size will be 0.2 or 20% of the entire data set, and the rest of the 80% of the data set will be used as training data set.

Day 6: Machine Learning Libraries

Machine learning libraries are sensitive routines and functions that are written in any given language. Software developers require a robust set of libraries to perform complex tasks without needing to rewrite multiple lines of code. Machine learning is largely based on mathematical optimization, probability, and statistics.

In the field of machine learning, Python is highly preferred credited to its consistent development time and flexibility. It is well suited to develop sophisticated models and production engines that can be directly plugged into production systems. One of its greatest assets being an extensive set of libraries that can help researchers who are less equipped with developer knowledge to easily execute machine learning. The Scikit-Learn library has evolved as the gold standard for the development of machine learning models with the use of Python, offering a wide variety of supervised and unsupervised ML algorithms. It is touted as one of the most user friendly and cleanest ML libraries to date. For example, decision trees, clustering, linear and logistics regressions and K-means. Scikit-learn uses a couple of basic Python libraries: NumPy and SciPy and adds a set of algorithms for data mining tasks including classification, regression and clustering. It is also capable of implementing tasks like feature selection, transforming data and ensemble methods in only a few lines.

In 2007, David Cournapeau developed the foundational code of Scikit-Learn during his participation in the "Summer of code" project for Google. Scikit-learn has become one of Python's most famous open source machine learning libraries since its launch in 2007. But it wasn't until 2010 that Scikit-Learn was released for public use. Scikit-Learn is an open sourced and BSD licensed, data mining and data analysis tool used to develop supervise and unsupervised machine learning algorithms build on Python. Scikit-learn offers various ML algorithms such as "classification", "regression", "dimensionality reduction", and "clustering". It also offers modules for feature extraction, data processing, and model evaluation.

Designed as an extension to the "SciPy" library, Scikit-Learn is based on "NumPy" and "Matplotlib", the most popular Python libraries. NumPy expands Python to support efficient operations on big arrays and multidimensional matrices. Matplotlib offers visualization tools and science computing modules are provided by SciPy. For scholarly studies, Scikit-Learn is popular because it has a well-documented, easy-to-use and flexible API. Developers are able to utilize Scikit-Learn for their experiments with various algorithms by only altering a few lines of the code. Scikit-Learn also provides a variety of training datasets, enabling developers to focus on algorithms instead of data collection and cleaning. Many of the algorithms of Scikit-Learn are quick and scalable to all but huge datasets. Scikit-learn is known for its reliability and automated tests are available for much of the library. Scikit-learn is extremely popular with beginners in machine learning to start implementing simple algorithms.

Prerequisites for application of Scikit-Learn library

The Scikit-Learn library is based on the SciPy (Scientific Python), which needs to be installed before you can use SciKit-Learn on your system. This stack involves the following:

- NumPy (Base n-dimensional array package)
- Matplotlib (Comprehensive 2D/3D plotting)
- SciPy (Fundamental library for scientific computing)
- IPython (Enhanced interactive console)
- SymPy (Symbolic mathematics)
- Pandas (Data structures and analysis)
- Seaborn (data visualization)

Installing Scikit-Learn
The latest version of Scikit-Learn can be found on "Scikit-Learn.org" and requires "Python (version >= 3.5); NumPy (version >= 1.11.0); SciPy (version >= 0.17.0); joblib (version >= 0.11)".

The plotting capabilities or functions of Scikit-learn start with "plot_" and require "Matplotlib (version >= 1.5.1)". Certain Scikit-Learn examples may need additional applications: "Scikit-Image (version >= 0.12.3), Pandas (version >= 0.18.0)". With prior installation of "NumPy" and "SciPy", the best method of installing Scikit-Learn is by utilizing "pip: pip install -U scikit-learn" or "conda: conda install scikit-learn". One must make sure that binary wheels are utilized with the use of the pip files and that "NumPy" and "SciPy" have not been recompiled from source, which may occur with the use of specific OS and hardware settings (for example, "Linux on a Raspberry Pi"). Developing "NumPy" and "SciPy" from source tends to be complicated (particularly on Windows). Therefore, they need to be setup carefully, making sure the optimized execution of linear algebra routines is achievable.

Application of machine learning using Scikit-Learn library

To understand how Scikit-Learn library is used in the development of machine learning algorithm, let us use the "Sales_Win_Loss data set from IBM's Watson repository" containing data obtained from sales campaign of a wholesale supplier of automotive parts. We will create a ML model to predict which sales campaign will be a winner and which will incur loss. The data set can be imported with the Pandas library and explored using Pandas techniques such as "head (), tail (), and dtypes ()". The plotting techniques from "Seaborn" will be used to visualize the data. To process the data Scikit-Learn's "preprocessing.LabelEncoder ()" will be used and "train_test_split ()" to separate the data set into training subset and testing subset. To generate predictions from our data set, three different algorithms will be used namely, "Linear Support Vector Classification and K-nearest neighbors classifier". To compare the performances of these algorithms Scikit-Learn library technique, "accuracy_score", will be used. The performance score of the models can be visualized with the use of the Scikit-Learn and Yellowbrick visualization tool.

Importing the data set

To import the "Sales_Win_Loss data set from IBM's Watson repository", first step is importing the "Pandas" module by executing the "*import pandas as pd*" command.

Then we leverage a variable url as "*https://community.watsonanalytics.com/wp content/uploads/2015/04/WA_Fn-UseC_-Sales-Win-Loss.csv*" for storage of the URL from where you will be downloading the dataset. Now, "*read_csv() as sales_data = pd.read_csv(url)*" technique will be used to read the above "csv or comma separated values" file, which is supplied by the Pandas module. The csv file will then be converted into a Pandas data framework, with the return variable as "*sales_data*", where the framework will be stored.

For new 'Pandas' users, the "*pd.read csv()*" technique in the code mentioned above will generate a tabular data structure called "data framework", where an index for each row is contained in the first column, and the label / name for each column in the first row are the initial column names acquired from the data set. In the above code snippet, the "*sales data*" variable results in a table depicted in the picture below.

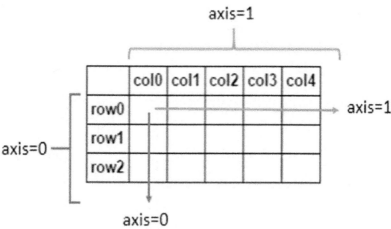

In the diagram above, the "row0, row1, row2" represent the individual record index and the "col0, col1, col2" represent the names for individual columns or features of the data set. With this step, you have successfully stored a copy of the data set and transformed it into a "Pandas" framework!

Now, using the *"head() as Sales_data.head()"* technique, the records from the data framework can be displayed as shown below to get a "feel" of the information contained in the data set.

	opportunity number	supplies subgroup	supplies group	region	route to market	elapsed days in sales stage	opportunity result
0	1641984	Exterior Accessories	Car Accessories	Northwest	Fields Sales	76	Won
1	1658010	Exterior Accessories	Car Accessories	Pacific	Reseller	63	Loss
2	1674737	Motorcycle Parts	Performance & Non-auto	Pacific	Reseller	24	Won
3	1675224	Shelters & RV	Performance & Non-auto	Midwest	Reseller	16	Loss

Data Exploration

Now that we have our own copy of the data set, which has been transformed into a "Pandas" data frame, we can quickly explore the data to understand what information can tell can be gathered from it and accordingly to plan a course of action.

In any ML project, data exploration tends to be a very critical phase. Even a fast data set exploration can offer us significant information that could be easily missed otherwise, and this information can propose significant questions that we can then attempt to answer on the basis of our project.Some third-party Python libraries will be used here to assist us with the processing of the data so that we can efficiently use this data with the powerful algorithms of Scikit-Learn. The same *"head()"* technique that we used to see some initial records of the imported data set in the earlier section can be used here. As a matter of fact, *"(head)"* is effectively capable of doing much more than displaying data records and customize the "head()" technique to display only selected records with commands like *"sales_data.head(n=2)"*. This command will selectively display the first 2 records of the data set. At a quick glance, it's obvious that columns such as "Supplies Group" and "Region" contain string data, while columns such as "Opportunity Result", "Opportunity Number", etc. are comprised of integer values. It can also be seen that there are unique identifiers for each record in the' Opportunity Number' column. Similarly, to display select records from the bottom of the table, the *"tail() as sales_data.tail()"* can be used. To view the different data types available in the data set, the Pandas technique *"dtypes() as sales_data.dtypes"* can be used. With this information, the data columns available in the data framework can be listed with their respective data types. We can figure out, for example, that the column "Supplies Subgroup" is an "object" data type and that the column "Client Size By Revenue" is an "integer data type". So, we have an understanding of columns that either contains integer values or string data.

Data Visualization

At this point, we are through with basic data exploration steps, so we will not attempt to build some appealing plots to portray the information visually and discover other concealed narratives from our data set. Of all the available python libraries providing data visualization features, "Seaborn" is one of the best available options so we will be using the same. Make sure that python plots module provided by "Seaborn" has been installed on your system and ready to be used. Now follow the steps below, generate the desired plot for the data set:

Step 1 - Import the "Seaborn" module with the command *"import seaborn as sns"*.

Step 2 - Import the "Matplotlib" module with command *"import matplotlib.pyplot as plt"*.

Step 3 - To set the "background color" of the plot as white, use command *"sns.set(style="whitegrid", color_codes=True)"*.

Step 4 - To set the "plot size" for all plots, use command *"sns.set(rc={'figure.figsize':(11.7,8.27)})"*.

Step 5 – To generate a "countplot", use command *"sns.countplot('Route To Market', data=sales_data, hue = 'Opportunity Result')"*.

Step 6 – To remove the top and bottom margins, use command *"sns.despine(offset=10, trim=True)"*.

Step 7 – To display the plot, use command *"plotplt.show()"*.

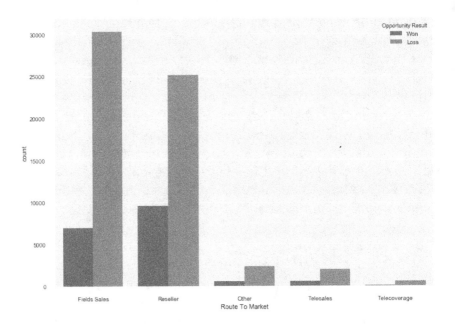

Quick recap - The "Seaborn" and "Matplotlib" modules were imported first. Then the *"set()"* technique was used to define the distinct characteristics for our plot, such as plot style and color. The background of the plot was defined to be white using the code snippet *"sns.set(style= "whitegrid", color codes= True)"*. Then the plot size was defined using command *"sns.set(rc= {'figure.figsize': (11.7,8.27)})"* that define the size of the plot as "11.7px and 8.27px".

Next the command *"sns.countplot('Route To Market',data= sales data, hue='Opportunity Result')"* was used to generate the plot. The "countplot()" technique enables creation of a count plot, which can

246

expose multiple arguments to customize the count plot according to our requirements. As part of the first *"countplot()"* argument, the X-axis was defined as the column "Route To Market" from the data set. The next argument concerns the source of the data set, which would be "sales_data" data framework we imported earlier. The third argument is the color of the bar graphs that were defined as "blue" for the column labeled "won" and "green" for the column labeled "loss".

Data Pre-processing

By now, you should have a clear understanding of what information is available in the data set. From the data exploration step, we established that majority of the columns in our data set are "string data", but "Scikit-Learn" can only process numerical data. Fortunately, the Scikit-Learn library offers us many ways to convert string data into numerical data, for example, *"LabelEncoder()"* technique. To transform categorical labels from the data set such as "won" and "loss" into numerical values, we will use the *"LabelEncoder()"* technique. Let's look at the pictures below to see what we are attempting to accomplish with the *"LabelEncoder()"* technique. The first image contains one column labeled "color" with three records, namely, "Red", "Green" and "Blue". By utilizing the *"LabelEncoder()"* technique, the record in the same "color" column can be converted to numerical values, as shown in the second image.

	Color			Color
0	1		0	Red
1	2		1	Green
2	3		2	Blue

Let's begin the real process of conversion now. Using the *"fit transform()"* technique given by *"LabelEncoder()"*, the labels in the categorical column like "Route To Market" can be encoded and converted to numerical labels comparable to those shown in the diagrams above. The function *"fit transform()"* requires input labels identified by the user and consequently returns encoded labels.

247

To know how the encoding is accomplished, let's go through an example quickly. The code instance below constitutes string data in form of a list of cities such as ["Paris", "Paris", "Tokyo", "Amsterdam"] that will be encoded into something comparable to "[2, 2, 1,3]".

Step 1 - To import the required module, use command *"from sklearn import preprocessing"*.

Step 2 – To create the Label encoder object, use command *"le = preprocessing.LabelEncoder()"*.

Step 3 – To convert the categorical columns into numerical values, use command:

"encoded_value = le.fit_transform(["Paris", "Paris", "Tokyo", "Amsterdam"])"

"print(encoded_value) [1 1 2 0]"

And there you have it! We just converted our string data labels into numerical values. The first step was importing the preprocessing module that offers the *"LabelEncoder()"* technique. Followed by the development of an object representing the *"LabelEncoder()"* type. Then the *"fit_transform()"* function of the object was used to distinguish between distinct classes of the list ["Paris", "Paris", "Tokyo", "Amsterdam"] and output the encoded values of "[1 1 20]". Did you observe that the *"LabelEncoder()"* technique assigned the numerical values to the classes in alphabetical order according to the initial letter of the classes, for example "(A)msterdam" was assigned code "0", "(P)aris" was assigned code "1" and "(T)okyo" was assigned code "2".

Creating Training and Test subsets

To know the interactions between distinct characteristics and how these characteristics influence the target variable, a ML algorithm must be trained on a collection of information. We need to split the complete data set into two subsets to accomplish this. One subset will serve as the training data set, which will be used to train our algorithm to construct machine learning models. The other subset will serve as the testing data set, which will be used to test the accuracy of the predictions generate by the ML model.

The 1st phase in this stage is separation of feature and target variables by following the steps below:

Step 1 – To select data excluding select columns, use command *"select columns other than 'Opportunity Number', 'Opportunity Result'cols = [col for col in sales_data.columns if col not in ['Opportunity Number','Opportunity Result']]"*.

Step 2 – To drop these select columns, use command *"dropping the 'Opportunity Number' and 'Opportunity Result' columns*
data = sales_data[cols]".

Step 3 – To assign the Opportunity Result column as "target", use command *"target = sales_data['Opportunity Result']*
data.head(n=2)".

The "Opportunity Number" column was removed since it just acts as a unique identifier for each record. The "Opportunity Result" contains the predictions we want to generate, so it becomes our "target" variable and can be removed from the data set for this phase. The first line of the above code will select all the columns except "Opportunity Number" and "Opportunity Result" in and assign these columns to a variable "cols". Then using the columns in the "cols" variable, a new data framework was developed. This is going to be the "feature set". Next, the column "Opportunity Result" from the *"sales_data"* data frame was used to develop a new data framework called "target". The second phase in this stage is to separate the date frameworks into trainings and testing subsets by following the steps below. Depending on the data set and desired predictions, it needs to be split into training and testing subset accordingly. For this exercise, we will use 75% of the data as training subset, and rest 25% will be used for the testing subset. We will leverage the *"train_test_split()"* technique in "Scikit-Learn" to separate the data using steps and code as below:

Step 1 – To import required module, use command *"from sklearn.model_selection import train_test_split"*.

Step 2 – To separate the data set, use command *"split data set into train and test setsdata_train, data_test, target_train, target_test = train_test_split(data, target, test_size = 0.30, random_state = 10)"*.

With the code above, the *"train_test_split"* module was first imported, followed by the use of *"train_test_split()"* technique to generate "training subset *(data_train, target_train)"* and "testing subset *(data_test, data_train)"*. The *"train_test_split()"* technique's first argument pertains to the features that were divided in the preceding stage; the next argument relates to the target ("Opportunity Result"). The third "test size" argument is the proportion of the data we wish to divide and use as a testing subset. For this example, we will busing 30% of the data for the testing subset, although this percentage share can vary as needed. The fourth 'random state' argument is used to make sure that the results can be reproduced every time.

Building the Machine Learning Model

The "machine_learning_map" provided by Scikit-Learn is widely used to choose the most appropriate ML algorithm for the data set. For this exercise, we will be using "Linear Support Vector Classification" and "K-nearest neighbors classifier" algorithms.

Linear Support Vector Classification

"Linear Support Vector Classification" or "Linear SVC" is a sub-classification of "Support Vector Machine (SVM)" algorithm, which we have reviewed in chapter 2 of this book titled "Machine Learning Algorithms". Using Linear SVC, the data can be divided into different planes so the algorithm can identify the optimal group structure for all the data classes. Here are the steps and code for this algorithm to build our first ML model:

Step 1 – To import the required modules, use commands *"from sklearn.svm import LinearSVC"* and *"from sklearn.metrics import accuracy_score"*.

Step 2 – To develop an LinearSVC object type, use command *"svc_model = LinearSVC(random_state=0)"*.

Step 3 – For training the algorithm and generate predictions from the testing data, use command *"pred = svc_model.fit(data_train, target_train).predict(data_test)"*.

Step 4 – To display the model accuracy score, use command *"print ('LinearSVC accuracy:', accuracy_score(target_test, pred, normalize = True))"*.

With the code above, the required modules were imported in the first step. We then developed a type of Linear SVC with the use of the *"svc_model"* object with "random_state" as '0'. The "random_state" command instructs the built-in random number generator for shuffling the data in a particular manner. In step 3, the "Linear SVC" algorithm is trained on the training data set and subsequently used to generate predictions for the target from the testing data. The *"accuracy_score()"* technique was used in the end to verify the "accuracy score" of the model, which could be displayed as "LinearSVC accuracy : 0.777811004785", for instance.

K-nearest Neighbors Classifier

The "k-nearest neighbors(k-NN)" algorithm is referred to as "a non-parametric method used for classification and regression in pattern recognition". In cases of classification and regression, "the input consists of the nearest k closest training examples in the feature space". K-NN is a form of "instance-based learning" or "lazy learning", in which the function is only locally estimated and all calculations are delayed until classification. The output is driven by the fact, whether the classification or regression method is used for k-NN:

- "k-nearest neighbors classification" - The "output" is a member of the class. An "object" is classified by its neighbors' plurality vote, assigning the object to the most prevalent class among its nearest "k-neighbors", where "k" denotes a small positive integer. If k= 1, the "object" is simply allocated to the closest neighbor's class.

- "k-nearest neighbors regression" - The output is the object's property value, which is computed as an average of the k-nearest neighbors values.

251

A helpful method for both regression as well as classification can be assigning weights to the neighbors' contributions, to allow closer neighbors to make more contributions in the average, compared to the neighbors located far apart. For instance, a known "weighting scheme" is to assign each neighbor a weight of "1/d", where "d" denotes the distance from the neighbor. The neighbors are selected from a set of objects for which the "class" (for "k-NN classification") or the feature value of the "object" (for "k-NN regression") is known.

Here are the steps and code for this algorithm to build our next ML model:

Step 1 – To import required modules, use command *"from sklearn.neighbors import KNeighborsClassifier"* and *"from sklearn.metrics import accuracy_score".*

Step 2 – For creation of object of the classifier, use command *"neigh = KNeighborsClassifier(n_neighbors=3)".*

Step 3 – For training of the algorithm, use command *"neigh.fit(data_train, target_train)".*

Step 4 – To generate predictions, use command *"pred = neigh.predict(data_test)".*

Step 5 – To evaluate accuracy, use command *"print ('KNeighbors accuracy score:', accuracy_score(target_test, pred))".*

With the code above, the required modules were imported in the first step. We then developed the object *"neigh"* of type "KNeighborsClassifier" with the volume of neighbors as *"n_neighbors=3".* In the next step, the *"fit()"* technique was used for training the algorithm on the dataset. Next, the model was tested on the testing data set using *"predict()"* technique. Finally, the accuracy score was obtained, which could be *"KNeighbors accuracy score : 0.814550580998",* for instance.

Now that our preferred algorithms have been introduced, the model with the highest accuracy score can be easily selected. In Scikit-Learn, we can utilize the "Yellowbrick library" for drawing comparison of the distinct models' efficiency visually, which offers techniques for depicting various scoring techniques visually.

Day 7: Neural Network Training With Tensorflow

TensorFlow can be defined as a Machine Learning platform providing end-to-end service with a variety of free and open sources. It has a system of multilayered nodes that allow for quick building, training, and deployment of artificial neural networks with large data sets.

It is touted as a "simple and flexible architecture to take new ideas from concept to code to state-of-the-art models and to publication at a rapid pace". For example, Google uses TensorFlow libraries in its image recognition and speech recognition tools and technologies.

Higher-level APIs such as "tf.estimator" can be used for specifying predefined architectures, such as "linear regressors" or "neural networks". The picture below shows the existing hierarchy of the TensorFlow tool kit:

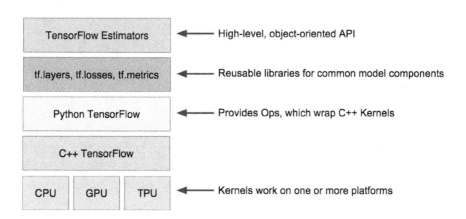

The picture shown below provides the purposes of the different layers:

Toolkit(s)	Description
Estimator (tf.estimator)	High-level, OOP API.
tf.layers/tf.losses/tf.metrics	Libraries for common model components.
TensorFlow	Lower-level APIs

The two fundamental components of TensorFlow are:

1. A "graph protocol buffer"
2. A "runtime" that can execute the graph

The two component mentioned above are similar to "Python" code and the "Python interpreter". Just as "Python interpreter" can run Python code on several hardware systems, TensorFlow can be operated on various hardware systems, like CPU, GPU, and TPU.

To make a decision regarding which API(s) should be used, you must consider the API offering the highest abstraction level to solve the target problem. Easier to use, but (by design) less flexible, are the greater abstract levels. It is recommended to first begin with the highest-level API and make everything work. If for certain unique modelling issues, you need extra flexibility, move one level down. Notice that each level is constructed on the lower level APIs. It should thus be quite simple to decrease the hierarchy. For the development of majority of Machine Learning models, we will use "tf.estimator" API, which significantly lowers the number of code lines needed for development. Also, "tf.estimator" is compatible with Scikit-Learn API.

The programming of computers needs a human programmer. Many lines of code are used by humans to instruct a computer to provide solutions to our problems. However, the computer can attempt to fix the issue itself through machine learning and neural networks. A neural network is "a function that learns the expected output for a given input from training datasets". For instance, you can train the neural network with many samples bear pictures to construct a neural network that recognizes pictures of a bear. The resulting network operates as functionality to generate the "bear" label as output for the bear picture input. Another more convenient example would be: training the neural network using multiple user activity logs from gaming servers and generate an output stating which users are very likely to convert to paying customer.

Unlike the "Artificial Neural Network" (explained in detail in Chapter 2 of this book), the "Neural Network" features only a single neuron, also called as "perception". It is a straightforward and fundamental mechanism that can be implemented with basic math. The primary distinction between traditional programming and a neural network is that computers running on neural network learn from the provided training data set to determine the parameters (weights and prejudice) on their own without needing any human assistance. Algorithms like "back propagation" and "gradient descent" may be used to train the parameters. It can be stated that the computer tries to increase or decrease every parameter a bit, in the hope that the optimal combination of Parameters can be found to minimize the error compared with training data set.

Fundamentals of Neural Network

- Neural networks need clear and informative big data to be trained. You can think of Neural networks as a toddler. They start by observing how their parents are walking. Then they attempt to walk on their own, and the kid learns how to accomplish future tasks with every step. Similarly, the Neural network may fail a few times, but it learns how to generate desired predictions after a few failing attempts.

- For complicated issues such as image processing, it is advisable to use Neural Networks. Neural networks belong to a group of algorithms called "representation learning algorithms". These algorithms are capable of simplifying complicated issues by generating simple (or "representative") form, which tends to be more difficult for conventional (non-representation) algorithms.

• To determine what type of neural network model is suitable for solving the issue at hand, let the data dictate how you fix the issue. For instance, "recurring neural networks" are more appropriate if the issue pertains to sequence generation. While it might be better for you to use "convolutional neural networks" to solve an image-related issue.

• In order to run a deep neural network model, hardware specifications are vital. Neural networks have been around for a long time now, but they are recently experiencing an upsurge primarily credited to the fact that computer resources today are better and more effective. If you want to address a real-life problem using a neural network, it is wise to purchase high-end hardware.

Training a Neural Network using TensorFlow

In this exercise, we will develop a model of neural networks for classifying clothing images such as sneakers and shirts using TensorFlow library.

I – Import the dataset

For this example, we will be using "Fashion MNIST" data set with 60,000 pictures representing 10 different categories. The low resolution pictures (28 to 28 pixels) indicate individual clothing items. For the classic MNIST dataset, "Fashion MNIST" is utilized as a "drop-in" replacement. The "MNIST" data set includes pictures of handwritten numbers (0, 1, and so on.) in the same format as the clothing items used in this example. To train the network, we will use 60,000 pictures, and 10,000 pictures will be used to assess the accuracy with which the network has learned how to classify pictures.

The "Fashion MNIST" data set is accessible directly from TensorFlow, using the import command as below:

"fashion_mnist = keras.datasets.fashion_mnist (train_images, train_labels), (test_images, test_labels) = fashion_mnist.load_data()"

After the dataset has been loaded system will return 4 different "NumPy arrays" including:

- The *"train_images"* and *"train_labels"* arrays, which serve as the "training dataset" for the model.
- The *"test_images"* and *"test_labels"* arrays, which serve as the "testing dataset" that the model can be tested against.'

Now we need to create labels for an array of integers (0 to 9), corresponding to each category/class of the clothing picture in the data set, using command below, which will look like the table represented in the picture below. This will be useful in generating predictions using our model.

"class_names = ['T-shirt/top', 'Trouser', 'Pullover', 'Dress', 'Coat', 'Sandal', 'Shirt', 'Sneaker', 'Bag', 'Ankle boot']"

Label	Class
0	T-shirt/top
1	Trouser
2	Pullover
3	Dress
4	Coat
5	Sandal
6	Shirt
7	Sneaker
8	Bag
9	Ankle boot

II – Data Exploration

By exploring the data set using the commands listed below, you will be able to get some preliminary sense of the data set:

To view the total no. of images in the "training data set" and the size of each image – "*train_images.shape*", which will produce the output displayed as "(60000, 28, 28)", stating we have 60,000 pictures of 28 to 28 pixel size.

To view the total no. of labels in the "training dataset" – "*len(train_labels)*", which will produce the output displayed as "60000" stating we have 60,000 labels in the training data set.

To view the data type of each label used in the "training dataset"– "*train_labels*", which will produce the output displayed as "*array([9, 0, 0, ..., 3, 0, 5], dtype=uint8)*" stating each label is an integer between o and 9.

To view the total no. of images in the "testing dataset" and the size of each image – "*test_images.shape*", which will produce the output displayed as "(10000, 28, 28)", stating we have 10,000 pictures of 28 to 28 pixel size in the testing data set.

To view the total number of labels in the "testing dataset" – "*len(test_labels)*", which will produce the output displayed as "10000", stating we have 10,000 labels in the testing data set.

III – Data Pre-processing

To make the data suitable for training the model, it needs to be pre-processed. It is essential to pre-process the data sets to be used for training and testing in the same manner.

For instance, you notice the first picture in the training data set has the pixel values between 0 and 255, by executing the commands below:

"*plt.figure()*" "*plt.imshow(train_images[0])*" "*plt.colorbar()*" "*plt.grid(False)*" "*plt.show()*"

These pixel values need to be scaled to fall between 0 to 1, prior to being utilized as input for the Neural Network model. Therefore, the values need to be divided by 255, for both the data subsets, using commands below:

"train_images = train_images / 255.0" "test_images = test_images / 255.0"

The final pre-processing step here would be to make sure that the data is is desired format prior to building the Neural Network by viewing the first 20 pictures from the training dataset and displaying the "class name" under each picture, using commands below:

"plt.figure(figsize=(10,10))" "for i in range(20):   plt.subplot(5,5,i+1)   plt.xticks([])   plt.yticks([])   plt.grid(False)   plt.imshow(train_images[i], cmap=plt.cm.binary)   plt.xlabel(class_names[train_labels[i]])" "plt.show()"

IV – Building the Neural Network Model
To build up the "Neural Network", the constituting layers of the model first need to be configured and only then the model can be compiled.

Configuring the layers
The "layers" are the fundamental construction block of a neural network. These "layers" take out information from the data entered, generating representations that tend to be extremely valuable addressing the problem. Majority of "deep learning" involves stacking and linking fundamental layers together. The parameters that are learned during practice are available in most of the layers, like "tf.keras.layers.Dense". To configure the required layers, use command below:

"model = keras.Sequential([keras.layers.Flatten(input_shape=(28, 28)),   keras.layers.Dense(128,

activation=tf.nn.relu),   keras.layers.Dense(10,
activation=tf.nn.softmax)])"

The *"tf.keras.layers.Flatten"* is the first layer in this network, which turns the picture format from a 2-dimesnional array of 28x28 size to a 1-dimension array with "28x28 = 784" pixels. Consider this layer as unchained rows of pixels in the picture that arranged these pictures but without any learning parameters and capable of only altering the data. The network comprises of couple of *"tf.keras.layers.Dense"* layers after pixels are flattened. These are neural layers that are fully or densely connected. There are 128 nodes or neurons in the first Dense layer. The succeeding and final layer is a ten node layer of *"Softmax"*, which generated an array of ten different probability scores amounting to "1". Every single node includes a probability score indicating that one of the ten classes is likely to contain the existing picture.

Compiling the model
Before being able to train the model, some final tweaks are needed to be made in the model compilation step, such as:

- Loss function— This provides a measure of the model's accuracy during training. This feature should be minimized so that the model is "directed" in the correct direction.

- Optimizer —These are the updates made to the model on the basis of the data it can view as well as its "loss function".

- Metrics — Used for monitoring the training and testing procedures. For example, the code below utilizes accuracy, measured by computing the fraction of the pictures that were classified accurately.

"model.compile(optimizer='adam',

loss='sparse_categorical_crossentropy',
metrics=['accuracy'])"

V – Training the Model

The steps listed below are utilized for training the "Neural Network Model":

- Feed the training data to the model, using "train_images" and "train_labels" arrays.
- Allow the network to learn the association of pictures and corresponding labels.
- Generate predictions using the model for a predefined test date set, for example, the "test_images" array. Then the predictions must be verified by matching the labels from the "test_labels" array.

You can begin to train the network by utilizing the "model.fit" method. To verify the system is a "fit" for the training data, use command "model.fit (train_images, train_labels, epochs=5)". The epochs are displayed as below, suggesting that the model has reached accuracy of around 0.89 or 89% of the training data:

"Epoch 1/5
60000/60000 [===================] - 4s 75us/sample - loss: 0.5018 - acc: 0.8241

Epoch 2/5
60000/60000 [===================] - 4s 71us/sample - loss: 0.3763 - acc: 0.8643

Epoch 3/5
60000/60000 [===================] - 4s 71us/sample - loss: 0.3382 - acc: 0.8777

Epoch 4/5
60000/60000 [===================] - 4s 72us/sample - loss: 0.3138 - acc: 0.8846
Epoch 5/5

*60000/60000 [====================] - 4s 72us/sample -
loss: 0.2967 - acc: 0.8897*

<tensorflow.python.keras.callbacks.History at 0x7f65fb64b5c0>"

VI – Measuring the accuracy of the Neural Network Model

To test the accuracy of the network, it must be verified against the testing data set by executing the commands below:

"test_loss, test_acc = model.evaluate(test_images, test_labels)" "print('Test accuracy:', test_acc)"

The output can be obtained as shown below, which suggests that the accuracy of the test result is around 0.86 or 86%, which is slightly less than the accuracy of the training data set. This is a classic example of "overfitting" when the performance or accuracy of the model is lower on new input or testing data than the training data.

*"10000/10000 [==============================] -
1s 51us/sample - loss: 0.3653 - acc: 0.8671*
Test accuracy: 0.8671"

VII – Generate predictions using the Neural Network Model

Now that our model has been trained sufficiently, we are ready to generate predictions from the model, by utilizing command *"predictions = model.predict (test_images)"*.

In the code below, the network has generated a prediction for labels of each picture in the testing data set. The prediction is generated as an array of ten integers with the "confidence" index for each of the ten categories (refer the import data stage) corresponding to the test picture.

"predictions[0]"
*"array([6.58371528e-06, 1.36480646e-10, 4.17183337e-08,
1.15178166e-10,*

8.30939484e-07, 1.49914682e-01, 3.11488043e-06, 4.63472381e-02,
6.10820061e-05, 8.03666413e-01], dtype=float32)"

To view the label with the highest "confidence" index, by utilizing command "np.argmax (predictions[0])".

A result "9", will suggest that the model has maximum confidence on the test image belonging to "class_names[9]" or according to our labels table, ankle boot.

To verify this prediction, use command "test_labels[0]", which should generate output as "9".

To view the whole set of predictions for the ten classes, use command below:

```
"def plot_image(i, predictions_array, true_label, img):
predictions_array,    true_label,    img    =    predictions_array[i],
true_label[i], img[i]   plt.grid(False)
  plt.xticks([])
  plt.yticks([])

  plt.imshow(img, cmap=plt.cm.binary)

  predicted_label = np.argmax(predictions_array)
  if predicted_label == true_label:
  color = 'blue'
  else:
  color = 'red'

  plt.xlabel('{}                                    {:2.0f}%
({})'.format(class_names[predicted_label],                10
0*np.max(predictions_array),

        class_names[true_label]),
            color=color)
```

```
def plot_value_array(i, predictions_array, true_label):
predictions_array, true_label = predictions_array[i], true_label[i]
plt.grid(False)
plt.xticks([])
plt.yticks([])
thisplot        =        plt.bar(range(10),        predictions_array,
color='#777777')
plt.ylim([0, 1])
predicted_label = np.argmax(predictions_array)

thisplot[predicted_label].set_color('red')
thisplot[true_label].set_color('blue')"
```

Now, for example, you may want to generate a prediction for a specific picture in the testing data set. You can do this by utilizing the command below:

```
"Grab an image from the test dataset
img = test_images[0]
print(img.shape)"
"(28, 28)"
```

To use the "tf.keras" models to generate this prediction, the picture must be added to a list, since these models have been optimized to generate predictions on a "collection of dataset" at a time. Use command below to accomplish this:

```
"# Add the image to a batch where it's the only member. img =
(np.expand_dims(img,0))
print(img.shape)"
"(1, 28, 28)"
```

Now, to generate the prediction for the picture by utilizing "tf.keras" use the command below:

```
"predictions_single = model.predict(img)
print(predictions_single)"
```

The predictions generated will resemble the code below:

"[[6.5837266e-06 1.3648087e-10 4.1718483e-08 1.1517859e-10 8.3093937e-07
   1.4991476e-01 3.1148918e-06 4.6347316e-02 6.1082108e-05 8.0366623e-01]]"

To generate a graph or plot for the prediction (as shown in the picture below), use command below:

"plot_value_array(0, predictions_single, test_labels)
plt.xticks(range(10), class_names, rotation=45)
plt.show()"

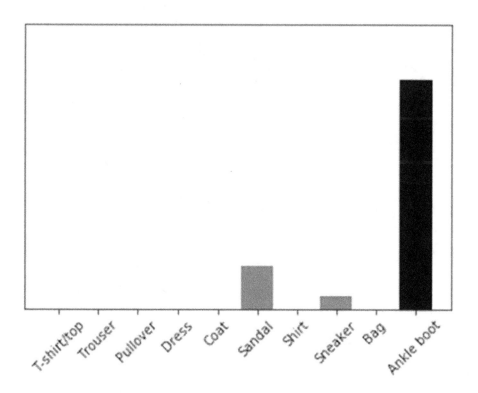

The *"model.predict"* generated the output as a "list of lists" for every single picture in the testing data set. To generate predictions specifically for the specific image, we used earlier, use command below:

"prediction_result = np.argmax(predictions_single[0])
print(prediction_result)"

The output or prediction generated should be "9", as we obtained earlier.

Ankle boot 80% (Ankle boot)

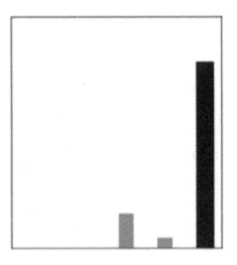

Python Machine Learning Conclusion

The next step is to make the best use of your machine learning knowledge that has significantly contributed to the creation of the "Silicon Valley" powerhouse. The use of machine learning technology has given rise to sophisticated machines, which are capable of studying human behaviors and activities in order to recognize any consistent patterns and generate predictions of products and services their consumers may be interested in. Under the shadow of their business model most futuristic businesses are gradually become technology firms with enterprise wide systems built upon machine learning algorithms. Consider some of the most innovative tech gadgets of the modern world that have been created in the past decade, such as "Amazon Alexa", "Apple's Siri", and "Google Home". The one aspect they all have in common is their underlying machine learning capabilities. Now that you have finished reading this book and mastered the use of Scikit-Learn and TensorFlow libraries, you are all set to start developing your own machine learning model by utilizing all the open sources readily available and explicitly mentioned in this book for that purpose.

www.ingramcontent.com/pod-product-compliance
Lightning Source LLC
LaVergne TN
LVHW022304060326
832902LV00020B/3272